UPSTAGED

UPSTAGED

MAKING THEATRE IN THE MEDIA AGE

ANNE NICHOLSON WEBER

Routledge
Taylor & Francis Group
New York   London

Published in 2006 by
Routledge
Taylor & Francis Group
270 Madison Avenue
New York, NY 10016

Published in Great Britain by
Routledge
Taylor & Francis Group
2 Park Square
Milton Park, Abingdon
Oxon OX14 4RN

© 2006 by Taylor & Francis Group, LLC
Routledge is an imprint of Taylor & Francis Group

Printed in the United States of America on acid-free paper
10 9 8 7 6 5 4 3 2 1

International Standard Book Number-10: 0-87830-185-2 (Hardcover) 0-87830-186-0 (Softcover)
International Standard Book Number-13: 978-0-87830-185-0 (Hardcover) 978-0-87830-186-7 (Softcover)

Library of Congress Cataloging-in-Publication Data

Catalog record is available from the Library of Congress

Taylor & Francis Group
is the Academic Division of Informa plc.

Visit the Taylor & Francis Web site at
http://www.taylorandfrancis.com

and the Routledge Web site at
http://www.routledge-ny.com

Contents

Acknowledgments

My thanks to:

Pauline Asper, Edward Bond, Greg Ripley-Duggan, Spalding Gray (posthumously), Michael Halberstam, Clare Lawrence, Anna Waterhouse, and David Winitsky, who generously contributed their time and ideas to a prior version of this project;

Andre Bishop, whose wise observations were eaten by a balky tape recorder;

Frank Rich and Stephen Dillane, for their insights and encouragement early on;

Francie Dickman, Georgina Calvert-Lee, and Judy Hertz, my writing buddies;

Susan Perry and Nancy Green, for friendly advice on the unfriendly proposal process;

Nancy Elan, Coty Sidnam and Derek Huntington, Richard and Linda Zuckerman, and Josh Freedman and Nina Steinberg, who cheerfully took me in whenever I turned up in London, New York, or Los Angeles;

Dianne Nelson and Diane Moore, for heroically deciphering interviews conducted next to espresso machines;

and Tom, who picked up wherever I left off.

Introduction

You know, you go to the theater. A character comes to the door. You think, Oh my God! He's going to cross the room. Jump cut, for Chrissake, just jump cut! And then, the next thing — oh, Christ, you just knew it! The bastard is going to sit down and *talk*.... And it's so slow. They do it so slowly. And the way they act! It's so old-fashioned. In these big barns and they have to shout. Why don't we admit it? It's been superseded. It had its moment, but its moment has gone.[1]

The character who delivers these lines in David Hare's play, *Amy's View*, is a young cinephile and aspiring filmmaker, a voice of the media age. The delicious irony, of course, is that he "shouts" these lines from the stage of one of those "big barns" to an audience of playgoers. What fun. And yet, for me — and, I suspect, for Hare — the question nonetheless hangs in the air: Why is this guy wrong?

Hare offers his answer in the form of the play. This book documents my efforts to answer the same question by asking others who would know.

The book was conceived during the 2000 Tony Awards broadcast. The Tony Awards ostensibly honor the heroes of Broadway, the symbolic capital of American theatre. Yet the show that year began with a song-and-dance number about stars who "started on Broadway" and made it all the way to Hollywood — as if the only hope of interesting audiences in the Tonys were to suggest that this year's honorees might eventually rate in Los Angeles. Television personality Rosie O'Donnell was the host. She spent most of her time dishing out lame sitcom humor and genuflecting to Hollywood. When Stephen Dillane received a Tony for his performance in Tom Stoppard's *The Real Thing* — a performance characterized by Sam Mendes as "one of the greatest I've ever seen"—the presenter was, of all people, talk show host Kathie Lee Gifford. She brightly delivered a homily about how the nominees should feel honored to follow in the footsteps of such Hollywood-certified stars as John Malkovich and Jeremy Irons. Watching Dillane accept his statuette and a photo-op kiss from Kathie Lee, I wondered whether he felt more celebrated or insulted.

For the last seventy-five years — since the introduction of the "talkies" in the '20s and television in the '50s — live theatre has struggled for its place in a culture increasingly dominated by the screen. How does that dominance affect individual theatre artists and theatrical movements? How does it affect what audiences seek from the theatre? What they can appreciate? In the end, what is the role of live theatre in a media-saturated culture?

An astonishing collection of generous people have given me their answers to these questions. Their only recompense will be my heartfelt gratitude, a copy of this book, and, I hope, some satisfaction in seeing gathered together in one place these many views of the landscape they inhabit. To state the obvious, they — not I — are the authors of this book.

Nonetheless, while every word and every idea in this book is the generous gift of someone else, my personal preoccupations no doubt come through. I chose to talk to people whose work I admire. Although I did not have a single list of questions, I did bring up certain topics over and over. And by editing the interviews, throwing out and rearranging material, I emphasized some ideas over others.

A word about methodology. The interviews were taped and transcribed. I then edited them quite substantially, both to take myself out and to reorganize what was often a rambling and wide-ranging conversation (always my preference) into a more focused and readable form. Participants were then given a free hand to edit the resulting transcript in order to correct distortions created by my meddling, to expand or clarify ideas, and — on occasion — to excise indiscretions. In every case, the text was improved by their changes.

Represented here are the ideas of twenty-four people who know various aspects of the theatre. No twenty-four people could possibly represent all of the English-speaking theatre, and these twenty-four are admittedly weighted toward the theatrical establishment. Some people I asked declined to be interviewed. And I didn't even ask many whose viewpoints would have been invaluable. Still, incomplete though it is, I hope that what is here is useful as an exploration of the problem of making a living versus making art; our increasing preference for images over words and for technology over the human body; and the need for theatre to play to its essential strengths — language, metaphor, immediacy, and community. Most of all, I hope this book more fittingly celebrates those strengths than did that ill-conceived Tony Awards show that so riled me five years ago.

Note

1. *Amy's View* by David Hare, reprinted with permission of Faber and Faber Ltd.

1
Nicholas Hytner

Nicholas Hytner has been the artistic director of Britain's National Theatre since April of 2003. This interview was conducted in London in March of 2001. Hytner was then a freelance director of theatre, opera, and film and was rehearsing a production of Shakespeare's The Winter's Tale *for the National Theatre, where most recently he has directed Alan Bennett's* The History Boys *and David Hare's* Stuff Happens. *His first film was* The Madness of King George, *which he had also directed for the stage and which was nominated for four Academy Awards. Subsequent films include* The Crucible.

Not Much Has Changed

One of the first things I'd say is that I'm not convinced that anything has happened recently that hasn't been happening since *The Jazz Singer* was released — or at least since people got televisions in their homes.

The movies did have a tremendous effect on popular theatre: variety died here and vaudeville died in the United States — though long after the movies achieved their dominance. But serious theatre has always been a minority activity, always. And I think probably classical theatre, serious theatre, what you might call art theatre, has been better served in recent decades than it was — as far as one can tell from reading about it — in the golden decades before the war. Of course, I think always 95 percent of what we do in theatre isn't excellent. But there is more of it now; actors are being better trained, directors are being better trained. One of the twentieth century's explosions of energy in British playwriting — the age of Barker and Shaw and Barrie — was pre-movies, but others in the '50s and '60s and the one in the '90s, are post-movies.

And there has also always been theatre which spends as much as it can in order to make as much as it can — theatre at the technological cutting edge. I can't remember which Gilbert and Sullivan operetta it was, but its main selling point was that it was lit by electricity. D'Oyly Carte made a huge song and dance about presenting it in the first theatre in London lit by electricity. I don't think much changes there either.

Bad Theatre/Bad Films

For reasons I've never quite got to the bottom of, bad theatre is intolerable, but bad films aren't. I suspect it's because bad movies are usually bad because they aim so low and, aiming low, they much more often than not achieve low, and so there is at least a sense of surface integrity. A movie which aims high and actually fails to get there is as painful as bad theatre. A pretentious art movie that doesn't make it is just as painful.

Also, a bad movie can hit you with such a barrage of sensory massage to distract you from how bad it is that you can get through it. Although you're perfectly well aware when writing and acting is bad in the movies, there are usually compensations. At least it's always audible. And you can shove any amount of stuff at a movie that isn't working to make it seem as if it is.

You can't do that in the theatre. With theatre, there is nothing technically to disguise bad acting or bad writing. Bad actors speaking ill-written dialogue — there's nothing you can do to distract attention from that. And also you're embarrassed as an audience member because you're there with them. Because the actors are looking at you, because they can see you, you're exposed in the theatre in a way you simply aren't in the movies.

The Future of Film

It's not been a relentless one-way process towards commercialism in the movies. Outside Hollywood, marvelous things still happen. Hollywood becomes increasingly irrelevant except to the vast corporations whose sole aim is profit. And even there, in the '70s, the directors made a bid for dominance, briefly. It didn't work. The studios are much more in control again, but are they more in control than they used to be when the studio system was in operation? Probably not.

Who knows what's going to happen now when sixteen-year-old kids can go out with commercially available little camcorders and commercially available software for their own computers and make movies in their own bedrooms of equivalent technical quality and put them on the Internet? What will start to happen soon — there are rare instances already — is that movies made in that way will occasionally find a distributor because they're so good.

Making Films

I made films because I was given the opportunity to and it was a creative challenge which seemed exciting and scary. And because it is tremendous to feel that the work you do can be seen globally. But essentially I did it because I was fascinated by the formal challenge. I did it because I had directed the play upon which my first film, *Madness of King George*, was based, and I was given the chance, and, having been an avid cinema-goer all my life, I wanted to see whether I could do it.

It was absolutely fascinating, but I don't think that I found out anything that people haven't found out before. One of the things I found out is that the kind of movie I like has a great deal in common with the theatre. It has dialogue which isn't necessarily an uninflected and accurate representation of the way we speak when we are not being observed. Or maybe it's not so much the kind of movie I like as the kind of movie I do. The kind of movie I *can* do — the kind of movie I would *like* to do, put it this way — shares with the theatre fully and richly developed character and imaginatively written dialogue. I'm more interested in hearing an actor bringing his or her skills to bear on properly written, beautifully wrought dialogue in order to make it feel utterly natural, than I am in hearing people speak the way they speak.

Obviously you can provide information, you can push the story forward, by moving a camera, by cutting from one shot to another. There is the delight after years in the theatre in realizing that the tedious stuff, the exposition — which is very, very hard to keep buoyant, which even Shakespeare has problems with — you can deal with in different ways. There is something tremendously exciting about being able to reveal character, reveal content, reveal story through image rather than through dialogue. Obviously you can do that in the cinema as a director controlling absolutely an audience's point of view in a way you can't in the theatre.

But on the other hand, you miss the challenge of the utterly democratic space that the stage provides, and you miss the challenge of making sure that a thousand people are looking at exactly the right thing at exactly the right moment, every night, even though they can look wherever they want. The challenges are different but equivalent. But there is something special about being in the same room as the people who are telling you the story; there is something special about being in the same room as the actors.

And of course a movie has a much more fixed meaning than a play, just because a movie can't take you by surprise in the same way since it can't take itself by surprise. A movie can't take itself by surprise because it's done. But a play, every time it's performed, is a succession of unexpected surprises to everybody involved.

Metaphorical/Literal

When a movie takes you to Jane Austen's Bath, you are being asked to believe that this is what Bath was like, this is a real world, they really were like this. Whereas I don't think that ever happens to the same extent on the stage because you're always aware of being in the same room, now, as these people on a stage. A stage, even when it's a kitchen, implies something more than a kitchen, because you know — I'm talking about barely conscious processes now, but you know — that what you're involved in here is a conspiracy to make this a kitchen, and therefore you assume that it's a lot more than a kitchen. There's always a metaphorical element to a stage; it always counts for something more.

Few movies try for that. A movie will take you to Bath c. 1810, and that's what it tells you to believe it is. The language of film storytelling, however, is much less literal than its representation of reality: it involves very, very selective points of view and this odd language of cutting wide shot to close-up — why? — and from close-up to close-up. It's a very odd language, although now we've all universally accepted it. As part of the language, as part of the apparatus, the movies offer us a highly elaborate, very artificial way of looking at the world — camera moving, cut, cut. But the movie tells us that the world it is looking at does exist, did exist, or might exist. It's rarely asking you to fill in the gaps by bringing your own imagination to bear on it. As soon as you're asked to fill in the gaps, the gaps have resonance.

Nontraditional Casting

It's because movies are, by and large, more literal that nontraditional casting hasn't found favor in film. In the movie world, it's always, "This is real." Even if it's a spaceship, it's a real spaceship, and if the spaceship contains men and women of different racial backgrounds, that's because the spaceship contains men and women of different racial backgrounds; the movie is making that statement.

Nor should nontraditional casting always be expected to work in the theatre, in my view. I'm now speaking in too banal and simplistic a way about how a stage world creates itself but, to oversimplify, in the theatre you have an opportunity to locate your world at any distance from the real world. You can locate it relatively close to the real world; you can write a play and present a play that works quite hard to be a literal image of a literal place, a literal time — this is a real kitchen, in real Clapham in 2001 — in which case you have to cast traditionally. Even if race is not the subject, if it's about a family tearing itself to bits in a kitchen in Clapham in 2001, you can't sling an Asian into that family unless you want to say quite literally that one of the family is Asian.

Whereas, to take another example and an easy one, when I did a production of the old musical *Carousel*, which played London and New York, there were those who objected because I cast a number of black actors in roles that are traditionally white. For instance, in New York, Carrie Pipperidge — and there's a New England name if there ever was one — was played by an African American actress. People objected to the idea of a black girl marrying a white man in a time and place where that wouldn't have happened. To which I wanted to say, "If you can demonstrate to me that, at moments of great joy, New England fishing communities used to dance classical ballet in the street, I will recast this."

What I'm saying, giving you an example, elaborately, is that a musical usually locates its world at a metaphorical distance from the real world. So you can cast it any way you like.

Another example: *Madness of King George*, stage and screen. The possibility of nontraditional casting crossed my mind, but I thought, "I can't do this." The point of this play is it presents to you an accurate image of the English court in 1789. This is what it was like: here's the king, here's the court, here's the government. Indeed, there are scenes, bits of dialogue, which were reproduced from contemporary records, from the parliamentary debate, verbatim. If it had been a grand verse play in the tradition of *King Lear* — also a play about a king descending into madness — it might have been less literal and open to different casting possibilities (though less open to the more literal demands of a film). So I think nontraditional casting is an aesthetic issue as much as it is a political issue.

Musicals

Similarly, although musicals can work on film, current fashions in film make it harder. To negotiate the passage from speech to song, and from walking down the street to dancing down the street, is always tricky. And it's much harder to negotiate in a movie now because acting has become, for want of a better word, more naturalistic.

The MGM musicals of the '50s are, many of them, absolutely wonderful. They seem more extremely of themselves, more the essence of '50s Hollywood, than the '50s Hollywood films that aren't musicals. Plainly, back in the '50s and earlier, the way dialogue was written and said in general was more like the way dialogue was written and said in a musical. But movie musicals are harder to do now because the more naturalistic an audience requires its acting to be, the harder it is to move from dialogue to song. It just happens to be the way movies are at the moment. That's one reason so many musicals now take the easy way out and through-compose. If everything is sung, it's easier. None of the Vincent Minnelli movie musicals tries to do that.

What's happened on Broadway is quite different. Not long after the war, at the very time that rock and roll achieved its cultural dominance, the world of theatre music and the world of popular music just went off in different directions. There was a brief time, and only a brief time, when popular music and show music seemed to be occupying the same world, when Cole Porter was providing the standards. But it's been a long time since a stage show provided a standard. It has become increasingly difficult to write popular musical theatre of merit and sophistication without in some way looking backward. And that's to do with the different journeys that the musical worlds have taken.

The Theatre Audience Must Work

You can never just sit back and let a play come to you. You have to agree to take part, or it won't happen. We've all had the experience (an experience which, by the way, the theatre critics consistently deny the possibility of) of going to the theatre for some reason feeling out of sorts — you had an argument with your partner, or, if you work in the theatre, this particular actor once threw a glass of red wine at you at a party — and therefore not making the effort to come to the play. So that something which everybody else is generally entranced by, you don't understand. You think, "Am I the only stupid one or are they stupid?" You come out thinking, "No, I'm not stupid," because it's too painful to address the possibility that what is wrong is you. But the theatre will only work if the audience agrees to work too.

The wider public is more and more spoon fed and molly coddled. That has happened since the advent of talking movies with *The Jazz Singer*. If you look at the people who made the great movies of the '30s, more of them were theatre actors, they were all theatre writers, and a lot of them were theatre directors — and they all assumed that the audience would do more work.

Now the movies come to you. And one of the reasons for the success of the big pop operas in the '80s was that they also came to you; you didn't have to sit forward to come to them. The sound systems for those musicals have a not dissimilar effect to the sound systems in a contemporary movie house. And so they were big theatrical experiences that demanded less of an audience than the theatre usually does. They absolutely came to you. It's just easier.

Theatricality

Throughout the history of the theatre, theatre artists have wanted to provoke their audience using alienating devices such as masks, boys playing girls, dance, verse dialogue — devices which quite plainly do not produce a literal image of the world outside. They say, "This isn't the real world. This is a poetic image of the real world through which we can agree to discover stuff about the real world" — exactly the same way as if I am a Shakespeare heroine, I have to put on man's clothes, to be not myself, in order to discover who I am and where I fit in the world. What we're doing here is conspiring together: let's make our world not the real world in order to discover what the real world is like.

I don't think this is a feature of film as a form, but it is of the stage. And over and over again, you see theatre artists pushing this as hard as they can. What flashes in my mind is an example from the play I'm working on at the moment, *The Winter's Tale*. I've not counted them, but seven or eight times in the last act, in preparation for his final *coup* when the statue of Hermione comes to life, Shakespeare has someone say, "This is like an old tale," "This is a mouldy old tale," "This is like an old tale still," "If this were shown you on the stage you'd hoot at it." He keeps insisting, "What I'm showing doesn't make any sense. It's not real," drawing attention to the unreality of it, because he's written thirty-five plays by now and he knows that we will believe and, in fact, that the more that he tells us that we won't believe, the bigger the shock and the huger and more resonant the thrill when we do. And at the end of an evening, the more you feel that you've achieved something — that something has been required of your imagination and you've given it — the better you feel. Always.

2
Wallace Shawn

Wallace Shawn is an American playwright and actor. His film and television roles include My Dinner with André, *which he wrote with costar André Gregory, and* Vanya on 42nd Street, *both directed by Louis Malle; Woody Allen's* Manhattan *and* Radio Days; The Princess Bride; Toy Story *and* Toy Story 2; *and recurring appearances on* Star Trek: Deep Space Nine. *His plays include* Marie and Bruce, *which, after this interview in the summer of 2000, was made into a film directed by Tom Cairns and starring Julianne Moore and Matthew Broderick;* Aunt Dan and Lemon; The Designated Mourner, *which had previously been filmed by David Hare; and* The Fever, *which was also filmed after this interview in a version starring Vanessa Redgrave, directed by Carlo Gabriel Nero.*

A Place in the Theatre

I used to truly believe in myself as a playwright. There were various people who said to me in my early days, "Your plays are not good," and I fought with them. The great Martin Esslin, who invented the phrase, "theatre of the absurd" — an important intellectual of the theatre — attacked me, saying my plays were rubbish. I fought back. I argued. I said, "No, you're just not getting it and some day everyone will recognize that they're good." Now I would just say that I have no idea; maybe they're good, maybe they're absolutely worthless. I really don't know.

I'm fortunate that my plays have somehow made their way to a lot of people. I don't know how they found them, but they found them. My plays are also done in other countries. And I've also been able to make a living as an actor. So on my good days I feel very blessed. I really do. But I have no strong institutional loyalty to the "American theatre," in part because I'm on the outside of it. When American theatre people get together to talk, they don't talk about me. They don't invite me to join the conversation. I'm just not involved. I've devoted my life to writing plays, but my plays are not exactly accepted; and I can be bitter about that.

I do understand why my plays are not accepted, though. And looking at it from a certain point of view, I'm grateful that I've been as appreciated as I have been. But I've never had a commercial production of any of my plays, and I don't remember when a regional theatre in America last did a play of mine. Steppenwolf did, but it's been quite a while. Why should they? The people who go to the plays aren't interested.

It sounds snobbish of me to say, and not very attractive, but it is just a fact that the core New York audiences, certainly, and maybe the audiences of most regional theatres in America are not necessarily the best possible people on earth to enjoy my plays. There's a lack of liveliness in the core bourgeois theatre audience that is depressing. They're not hungry for an experience of the kind that my plays provide. My plays take a sort of effort; the audience has to actually listen to them.

There are a handful of people who could respond to my work, but it's very hard to assemble those people — to let them know that the thing that you're doing is what they're looking for. I did get a great audience for *The Fever* in New York somehow — maybe by getting an almost unbelievably negative review in the *New York Times*. I don't know how that worked. But those were pretty amazing people who came.

I performed it in five different theatres and didn't have a problem getting an audience, because I did it in small theatres for a very short run. If it had been a commercial enterprise, the *New York Times* review definitely would have killed it, and it did kill it in the sense that people in the rest of the country didn't think of putting it on. But somehow great people found their way to it — people who were willing to meet me halfway and really put in an effort to go on the journey with me.

Magical Lying

There's a magical aspect to theatre that is not present in movies, and that seems to be the thrill that keeps me going. While I know that a lot of the amazing feats that happen in a film are real and the actors actually did risk their necks, when you see it in a movie you assume that it's a trick, whether it is or not. For example, you don't want to see a movie of a magic show. The thrill of seeing a card trick is that the person has done it in front of your eyes — it's thrilling, amazing, you don't know how it's possible. If you see a card trick in a movie, it's just not that kind of feat: a card trick in a movie is almost meaningless.

So, similarly, I love the fact that in the theatre the actors are just like you and you're sharing the same space. The actor can suddenly start talking and actually fool you into believing that they're someone else and that there's this whole other situation unfolding in front of you. It's incredibly skillful lying, and it's a thrilling trick to see someone lie so unbelievably persuasively. It's like being in on the experience of an Anthony Blunt or Donald Maclean or Guy Burgess — spies who lived as regular Englishmen but who all the time were dissembling with incredible skill. In a play, you see that magnificent lying and you yourself are fooled by it. And they do it not just for a few minutes but for hours on end without making a mistake. Now that's amazing.

And then, on the other hand, there's truth involved, because the actors are actually encountering each other and there's a real relationship that you see between them — so very fascinating and exciting.

Those things don't happen on film; there's too much trickery interposed. Watching a film, you know that they created it over a long period, using all kinds of tricks, and of course that magic is lost.

Size of Expression

There are other things the theatre can do that movies can't do that I care about. For example, the extremes of human feeling and passion really don't come off too well on film because — how can I put this? — when people become truly obsessed, their behavior becomes theatrical. You don't need a close-up of screaming, yelling, or crying, because those forms of expression are already too big for film. They're theatrical. And when you see yelling and screaming and crying in films, you're too close to it and it's either too loud or it's unnaturally quiet; you're too aware of the microphone and you're too aware of the camera. It's very, very hard to make that stuff work on film. While the opposite is also true: casual interchanges can seem grotesque in a play, as when people are shouting hello at each other.

Being an Audience

I myself suffer from the problem that I only like theatre from a good seat. I've been spoiled like a lot of people by watching movies and television, where you can see very well and you can hear what the actors are saying. It's really, really hard for me to sit in row HH and not be able to see the faces of the actors and have to either strain to hear their voices or listen to projected voices which I know are grotesquely unnatural and which make it absolutely impossible for me to take the whole thing seriously. So I'm not a theatre person in that sense.

But I have had thrilling experiences in the theatre that I found deeply wonderful. One that certainly rushes to mind is the play that Charles Ludlam and Everett Quinton of the Ridiculous Theatrical Company did — the two-man play called *The Mystery of Irma Vep*. In a way, there couldn't have been anything more trivial than that play. I suppose you could call it a spoof of a Victorian melodrama, in which these two guys played twenty-five different characters. They had two chairs and a screen. They rehearsed and rehearsed and rehearsed and somehow, over the course of months or maybe years of rehearsal, they figured out how to change costumes behind that screen instantaneously. A guy in a tuxedo could walk at an ambling gait behind the screen and come out as the Duchess dressed in robes, furs, jewels. It was impossible, what was happening in front of your eyes. Obviously this alone was just a device; it was the acting which was so thrilling and so magical and inspired. There couldn't be a more trivial script, if you want to look at it that way, but as a theatre piece it was just something sublime that made you feel that life was worth living.

In their very beings, these guys stood for something. They were serious people who happened to be devoted to this idea of the ridiculous; they made it almost a religion. And, in a sense, Charles Ludlam literally died for his belief in frivolity. He was a nonbourgeois gay man who literally died because of the way that he lived, which was theoretically trivial and for fun. And he did these plays that were not serious; but they were sublime, you know, and I'm still inspired just by thinking about it.

By contrast, there's something absolutely horrible about seeing the kind of theatre that involves a lot of hypocrisy and fantasy where you are not fooled or taken in. To see a play where the actors are knocking themselves out to say lines truthfully that are, in themselves, not really good; or to see dancers in a musical trying to make you feel that they are loving the experience of dancing when actually you feel that either they're whipped dogs performing just to get the check or that they've deluded themselves into believing that it's wonderful when deep down they know better — that's terrible.

I don't really go to musicals. It's too upsetting to me. I literally become anguished when I see the actors panting and sweating to earn their paycheck or the approval of the audience. The Broadway audience loves to see the actors working unbelievably hard. The more physical energy the actors are putting out, the more the audience is impressed; they adore that. But to me that's horrible. I like to see relaxed people on stage. Twyla Tharp's dancers have to do incredibly difficult things, and it must be painful, but, because of their training and their discipline, I still feel a relaxation rather than a tension, even though they're doing feats way beyond what Broadway dancers do. They're liberating themselves somehow, whereas often the Broadway dancers seem to be enslaving themselves.

In any case, I'm somewhat skeptical of my own judgments of the work of others. I notice, for example, that people frequently disparage the work of their own countrymen. If you go to Sweden, you'll meet people who say, "Hey, Ingmar Bergman, he stinks. There are ten Swedish directors who are greatly superior." If you go to England, you'll meet people who say, "Mike Leigh, he's the twelfth best filmmaker in England. But have you ever heard of so-and-so?" If you go to India, you'll meet people who say, "Satyajit Ray, he stinks. He's terrible. He can't make a film to save his life. We have much better filmmakers than that." I totally believe that all those people are wrong. I *know* that Satyajit Ray and Ingmar Bergman and Mike Leigh are great filmmakers. So that makes me skeptical. If I was thrilled by something, that's because that person gave me something that I wanted and needed, and you can't argue with that. But if I'm left indifferent, I'm sometimes a little skeptical of myself.

Acting in Hollywood

A lot of people who work in theatre stumbled into it by accident. I don't know how many people there are who absolutely refuse to do film and who made committed decisions to be in theatre because they genuinely love theatre or are committed to certain values that they think have to do with theatre. I've met some. Certainly in England there are individuals who could perfectly well have been in television or film and who for artistic reasons preferred to work in theatre.

My film acting career started as a way to subsidize my writing, but I've done some things as an actor that have meant a lot to me. I've done some things as an actor that I didn't get much pay for, so you could hardly say they were subsidizing me. My work with André Gregory is something that has to be subsidized, not something that subsidizes anything else.

The people who own film studios are interested in profit. I haven't had much contact with the people at the very highest levels. They actually don't speak to actors. I've ridden on airplanes with some very high executives and they know who you are but they won't talk to you. They actually don't talk to actors; I think they consider actors almost contemptible in a funny way.

But the people who are on the lower rungs — whether someone who plays funny parts as a character actor, as in my case, or someone who is a makeup artist, or even someone who is a director — these are cogs in the machine, and I don't know if I can distinguish their values from those of people in the theatre. To take an example: I was in many episodes of *Star Trek*. When I think of the directors, the writers, the costume designers, the makeup artists, the actors — I draw a blank when I try to think of some difference between them and people who would put on one of my plays. I mean their commitment is 100 percent, their sincerity is 100 percent; they're pouring their heart and soul into it.

I decided long ago that I would draw distinctions in Hollywood. Some people might say it's all evil, but I decided that I wasn't going to see it that way. That's the choice I made about my life. Don't get me wrong. I do think most of what is produced out of Hollywood is propaganda for the American empire or whatever you want to call it, which is based on the exploitation of the oppressed. If you want to look at it that way, I'm the equivalent of the SS officer who, on the personal level, may be a very nice fellow. So of course most of it is evil and very harmful to the world, obviously — but for me that depends on the script. I read the script to decide whether I'm going to be involved in the first place. If I find the script evil, I don't do the project. But once I've accepted the script as something that I'm willing to be involved in, from then on it's pretty much the same as being in one of my own plays. I commit to it 100 percent.

Even if I could make a living as a playwright, I certainly would still have done *Star Trek* and *Clueless* and the Woody Allen films and Alan Rudolph's film and a few of the other Hollywood things that I've done. With *Star Trek*, for example, I would do it partly because the experience was amazing. It was like an incredible sporting event. You had to be inspired. You had to do it with no rehearsal. You had to just leap for it, which is totally contrary to my slow, deliberate rhythm of life and, for that very reason, it is particularly exciting.

Rehearsal

In film you're hoping for one great moment of inspiration when you will magically come up with something remarkable. And I think both film actors and film directors know that rehearsing for an hour or a day runs the risk of wasting the forces that are needed to produce that one moment of inspiration without really replacing them with anything else.

I've rehearsed *The Master Builder* of Ibsen with André Gregory since 1997, and we're now beginning to reach the point where certain moments occur somewhat spontaneously that just weren't possible in 1997 or even a year ago. But rehearsing a very emotional scene for an hour or a day, for example, could be dangerous, because that is not enough time.

Three movies that I've been involved in — *My Dinner with André, Uncle Vanya on 42nd Street,* and *The Wife,* directed by Tom Noonan — couldn't have been done if we just walked in and tried to do it; they would have been terrible. But we didn't rehearse for just a few weeks; we rehearsed for many, many months in each case. We got to know the material so well that inspiration somehow comes in a different way, and actually it can be more deeply felt than if you just walked in off the street. I do think there's always a great benefit to familiarity with the material, although even that is disputed by some film people because, for instance, people say James Stewart was benefited by the fact that he didn't know his lines and he was struggling to remember them and he looked to the audience as if he was just very natural. I don't know if that's true. But personally, I'm not afraid of rehearsals.

With the exception of the Ridiculous Theatrical Company, I hold all acting to the standard of good film acting, which is very simple: you're supposed to believe that it's really happening. And if you see Bob DeNiro or Gerard Depardieu or Mike Leigh's films, you believe everything that people are saying and doing. You just totally believe that it's real. And that's true even of a lot of television acting. Stylewise, Roseanne Barr is completely believable. So, that's the standard that we walk around with. When you go to a play you expect to believe it in that same way, and sometimes you do and sometimes you don't.

When I've acted in the theatre with André Gregory, we've rehearsed for a very long time. And that allows us to fool people even if the audience is sitting pretty close to us. But then that type of theatre — long rehearsals and small audiences — is the end of theatre because it can't be sustained. How can that pay for itself? I love acting with the intimacy that is possible in film and also in the weird kind of theatre that I do, which is, as I say, a dead end. That's why we wanted to make a movie of *Uncle Vanya* and why we hope to make a movie of *The Master Builder* — because we want more people to see it.

Filming the Plays

For the same reason, I have this eternal interest in putting my own plays on film. Both *The Fever* and *Marie and Bruce* are films which we hope may be made. If they happen, they won't be the plays, though; they'll be something else.

The film of *The Designated Mourner* was in many ways like the play. The play was rehearsed and performed and then filmed when the performances were over. And even so, it was different. The film is a more frank and unforgiving examination of the people. In the play, the character of Jack was able to charm and fool the audience more easily because he was at a distance and he could manipulate them. In the film, he's pinned, and his scary characteristics are more visible. And I would say of the character of Judy that her quiet credibility comes through more strongly in the film; on stage, she was sometimes hidden by the amusingness of Jack.

I've collaborated on the screenplays of *The Fever* and *Marie and Bruce* with the directors of those two films. That was very enjoyable. The question of how you make a good film out of a play is very interesting and quite entertaining to think about. I've had great fun.

And the thought that people outside the little circle of theatregoers might see them is great. There is a kind of excitement about film. The movie audience in many cases is livelier. Movies are for everybody; you don't even know who goes to them. And then they get put on television and they're even more accessible.

There's a wonderful actor who was in a play of mine who lived in a poor Mexican community in Texas when he was growing up. He had access to a public TV station when he was a teenager, and he happened on the movie of *Marat-Sade*. He saw that movie and he didn't know what in the world it was; he had no idea. But he just knew that this seemed to be true. He was suddenly looking at something that seemed like life to him. And that moment changed his life. He wasn't looking for it; it was just there on the TV.

So that is something that you hope for, that you dream of. It's quite exciting, that thought, as opposed to trying to convince people who don't really like what you do that they should like it. Why bother? A movie can find its audience; it has time to find its audience and it can go anywhere. For that reason, I'm dying to have my work made into films.

3
Simon Callow

Simon Callow is a highly regarded British actor, director, and writer. A fixture of the English stage, he has also acted extensively in film and television, in such roles as Reverend Beebe in A Room with a View, *Gareth in* Four Weddings and a Funeral, *and Edmund Tilney in* Shakespeare in Love. *His numerous books about the theatre include biographies of Charles Laughton and Orson Welles, and autobiographical works about his life as a young actor* (Being an Actor) *and his relationship with the celebrated playwrights' agent, Peggy Ramsay* (Love Is Where It Falls). *At the time of this interview in March of 2002, Simon Callow was rehearsing a one-man show,* The Mystery of Charles Dickens, *for a production at the Old Vic.*

Mythmaking

We live in a very limited world. The nefarious nature of Hollywood is that it is essentially a commercial organization, so what it does is to recycle things: "On this occasion, that worked, so let's make some more of it and make some more money out of it."

All screenwriting courses talk about myth, and screen writers do indeed tell myths, but they're telling them with their conscious brain; they're thinking, "Now, if I add this element and that element, I'll get a myth." Many action movies are predicated on myth — the stories go back to the Odyssey — but they try to achieve the mythic by mechanical means.

But the way in which you engage with the myth is by encountering the subconscious. As far as actors are concerned, I'm talking about the sort of activity in which, for example, Charles Laughton was involved, or the younger Marlon Brando, who in their own persons, their own bodies, their own voices would incarnate a hidden world of inner experience: profound transformations, inner and outer. Other actors create an archetype of themselves: Bette Davis, Cary Grant, John Wayne, in their more or less fixed personalities embodying and intensifying certain quintessential human qualities. Among directors, Eisenstein or the Tarkovsky of *Andrei Rublev* and *Solaris,* or Renoir in *La Règle du Jeu,* all create consistent worlds of the imagination which transcend vulgar realism but which have their own profound sense of reality. They've all done this; they've created myths that are hugely poetic and haunt you and disturb you, just exactly as Rembrandt does when he paints his mother — taking a totally credible image of an old woman in Holland in the seventeenth century, but somehow penetrating into the nature of all old women, all women, all mothers. Somehow the archetype is uncovered. A whole strange energy comes out of that.

Each individual actor has within himself the possibility of that kind of real poetry and transformation. And in transforming himself, the actor can release things in the subconscious of the audience which are disturbing and exhilarating and life changing. But that will never happen if you primarily address yourself to the conscious mind.

Euthanasia

You must not imagine that I'm saying, "Theatre good, film bad." On the contrary, I love film; I think it is a great, great art form. What else could I think? The problem with film is that although there are just as many mediocre theatre productions as there are mediocre films, the mediocre theatre productions finish when they finish, whereas the films are there for all time. There used to be the kindly natural spontaneous euthanasia of nitrate stock, but now they last forever.

Rehearsal and Film Acting

The films I've most liked being in benefited hugely from having a rehearsal period. *Shakespeare in Love* had a rehearsal period; *Four Weddings and a Funeral* did. It wasn't a long period, just enough time for people to talk to each other, hear each other's voices, take the measure of each other, and so on. Generally speaking, though, films are not created like that. You just turn up on the set, you know your lines, you may have a tiny discussion with the director, most likely you won't, and you just plunge in, say something or not, and then do it again and again and again, and then stop. The world of the shoot is not a creative environment, because, idiotically, no one thinks it's very important. Or else, in some very odd way, they think it's bad form to actually work at it: we should all somehow just be able to do it.

Mike Newell, with whom I made *The Good Father* and *Four Weddings and a Funeral*, is quite different: he does work with you on the set. Mike started in television, at the BBC, and many of those English directors who came out of television — Stephen Frears, John Madden — do work on the set. They find time, you know. When they started at the BBC directing plays for television, you had three weeks of rehearsal and then you'd do the technical run of the whole screenplay, and then finally you'd have two days in the studio shooting as much as possible in chronological sequence. It was all very, very carefully prepared. Those were the circumstances in which they learned their craft.

People who went to film school have very different expectations. They assemble the elements and then let them happen. That way you often don't know what you've got until you actually put it all together, and the director realizes, "Oh that doesn't work. We'll have to do it some other way." But their objective is to shoot as much as they can to have stuff to play with. As an actor, you have to develop a rather different state of mind to work this way. You have to develop a sort of Buddhist resignation about it, saying "I'll give you whatever I can. And if it's useful to you, great, and if not, not."

In my view, the best of all acting performances in film are those in Ingmar Bergman's work. All of his films. Go right back to the early ones. *Sawdust and Tinsel. Winter Light.* Astounding. The actors are not only rich and full and true, but they're also not self-conscious about their character transformations. Max von Sydow plays one kind of character in one film and in the next he's radically different, completely transformed, has changed everything about himself, but entirely without drawing attention to it. This is the result of an entirely different working environment. First of all, Bergman's actors have worked together for many years; secondly, they've worked together in the theatre as well; thirdly, Bergman does them the honor, shows them the respect, of circulating among the actors his seminal thoughts in the form of a short story, which is the prototype of the screenplay, so that everyone is equally immersed in the story he intends to tell. They all know where the work is coming from. And the result is quite simply the greatest acting in the world.

The Blandishments and Rewards of Film Acting

I think most actors arrive at drama school with the ambition of being film actors. I think there are very, very few actors who think, "No, my place is in the theatre. That's where I'll be." Some wonderful actors turn out to be completely un-photogenic, so then they go back to the theatre and they stay in the theatre and that's the theatre's great gain. The rest of us who seem to have a reasonable relationship with the camera can find it very tough to resist its blandishments, you know.

But there are intrinsic rewards as well. I can do things on film that I can't do anywhere else. There's obviously a degree of intimacy you can achieve. And there are also things of extreme physical difficulty that you couldn't possibly do night after night. You can push yourself. You can risk losing your voice completely because you don't have to do it again. That's a lovely thing. The point about acting on the stage is that it entails — no matter how small the auditorium — an act of projection. But in movies it's different. You're not actually playing out there; the camera is witnessing you, it's absorbing you, taking you in. It's curiously more active than a theatre audience, whom you can dominate. You can never dominate the camera; you can only invite it in.

The New York/Hollywood Split

Film is a wonderful medium. Radio is another wonderful medium, and also recorded books. They're all wonderful, and there's absolutely no point whatever in choosing one over the other. It's easier to have an integrated career here in

England because London is the center of everything. In America, it's a straight split between New York for theatre and L.A. for film. As soon as that split came about, nothing was ever going to be the same again; the sort of integration that Bergman's actors experience was simply unavailable to an American actor. Actors who became successful on the stage were snapped up by Hollywood, and then moved to movie city and became movie actors — a strange concept in itself. People who live in Hollywood live this unreal life. It's probably because of the oddity of a whole city being dedicated to this one thing. It becomes rather rarified air in which to live. It's really quite a bizarre place.

The Secularization of Acting

In actors there is an interesting conjunction of the sacred and profane. Anybody who has allowed him- or herself to sense the power within them in relation to an audience knows that there's something weird going on there, that there are some big, big energies which have certain rules that we may or may not understand. I became conscious of the theatre and of acting at the very tail end of that famous flowering of the Oliviers and the Gielguds and Richardsons and Peggy Ashcrofts and so on, when actors felt a certain sense of destiny. They had a feeling that it was a responsibility and a glory being one of those elected to tell the story of the tribe, and they were very conscious of belonging to an unbroken tradition stretching back to Burbage, through Garrick, Mrs. Siddons, Henry Irving, and so on. There were financial rewards, and there was a certain attendant glamour, but most particularly there was a sense of doing something valuable and important and unique.

But now there's an idea that it's just a job, just a craft — get on with it. Your objective is ordinariness: that the man on the street becomes the man on the stage, the man on the stage becomes the man on the street. The idea is that you must be as like the audience as possible. It has to do with developments in society in general towards an allegedly more democratic world, and a morbid dread of elitism.

In England, some of this has its roots in the Royal Court Theatre in the late '50s and early '60s, where a whole new breed of actors came along to sweep away the perceived bourgeois cosiness which had anesthetized acting. The key word is "perceived." Whether Dame Edith Evans was actually bourgeois in her performances I rather doubt. Whether Laurence Olivier was bourgeois — I don't think so. He was all kinds of things, but not that. He was some sort of a restless, Marlovian figure who wanted to push acting further and further towards an overwhelming sensuous experience. But it was decreed that the charm school approach — the rather pampered, decadent environments in which actors were denatured and their natural class, accent, and all the rest of it was bred out of them — turned actors into these sorts of Binkie Beaumont luvvies of both sexes, and that, it was felt, had to stop.

There was something in that criticism, but look what we've lost. The possibility of poetry in acting is never given a chance. The net result of the Royal

Court revolution was unvarnished acting, acting which was plain and simple and honest. That kind of theatre is all about accurate representation of the observed human situation. And I don't think that's what acting is. I don't think that can be true of acting any more than it would be true of painting. It would be false to say that what we expect in painting is verisimilitude. We are allowed to play only three or four notes on the keyboard of the grand piano that is acting, and that saddens me, and I think it's very disappointing for the audience as well.

Imagination is no longer regarded as the primary element of theatre. I tread very carefully because in no sense am I intending to criticize my fellow actors, who work incredibly hard and indeed work on themselves very hard. But I think there's a serious problem in the conception of what an actor's work on him- or herself should really be. Of course there are technical skills and constant observation of the real world, but then there is also fantasy and a very personal contribution. Send a bucket right down into the well and bring something up which will haunt you. My theory is that the theatre is like a zoo. You go to see extraordinary people — that's why we bother to shell out our forty-five pounds or our eighty dollars for a ticket. You want to go see a Ralph Richardson or an Ethel Barrymore because they are extraordinary, because they tell the truth in a very interesting way. The job of acting is to be memorable. And nourishing. We want acting to be a banquet, not a snack. If you just want a Big Mac, then I suppose it fills a hole in your stomach — I wouldn't know.

Growing an Actor

Another thing that has very much disappeared, certainly as far as I've experienced it, is the sense of an actor's art being shaped throughout the course of a career. Many actors have a very alienated career; you do a job, bang, hup, finished, you're done with that, on to the next, with no sense of continuity whatever. Whereas the old producers like Binkie Beaumont would contract artists and then slowly build them up — this part, that part. The old actor manager companies, that was exactly what they did. And the Royal Shakespeare Company, Olivier's National Theatre. There was a conscious focus on a nurturing process, a challenging process, that sense that you're in training for something. The idea was that you would, in the Japanese attitude, take your natural endowments and shape them. Your natural endowments include not only your voice and your body but your personality — your personality being the key — and these had to be cultivated. As Micheál macLiammóir, the great Irish actor, said, "As a painter works off his palette and as a musician works off his keyboard and a whore works off her body, so the actor works off his personality." You develop its possibilities. You're trying to make yourself more and more expressive, more and more interesting, more and more watchable. You cultivate yourself. It's not a question of being self-conscious or narcissistic — the opposite, in fact, because you're looking outward.

Actors very much used to look at each other. They'd say, "Wow, that's what Tony does. Well, I can use that. I'll steal that. I'll find a way of doing that." It's not without its dangers. There was a generation of Olivier clones — you know, actors trying to be like Larry — but the problem was just that they didn't get beyond it. You have to go through it. You have to imitate. I don't have much sense that actors go see each others' work nowadays, and think, "God! I want to do that." They do say Robert DeNiro is great, but just, "Yeah, he's great, but I can't get anything from that. I can't learn from that. I must be original." As an artist of any kind, you have to relate to your predecessors and, indeed, your contemporaries, and think, "God, this is fantastic and interesting!" and then make it your own, take it on. Actors should be ambitious for their art, not just for their careers.

Cutting the Actor Down to Size

You have to understand that whenever anybody in England is even remotely successful, in whatever sphere, they have to be trashed, brought down to size. Actors who talk about acting and say that acting is difficult, that it's perhaps a serious job, an interesting one — that attitude is held up to ridicule by certain journalists and indeed certain members of the profession. They really like to believe that acting is just a trick, the central elements of which are learning your lines and not bumping into the furniture. There's a sense that actors are "jammy buggers," as we say in England, who are hideously overpaid, their opinions are always being canvassed, they're all indulgent tossers, and that what you should really do as an actor is be seen, be filmed, and then shut up. But it's totally hypocritical because it's the newspapers who pursue actors everywhere in the hope of catching them out in their personal lives or in their utterances. They're forever trying to chip away at them, punishing them for the audacity of daring to stand on a stage and ask to be looked at.

I was reading a speech of Dickens's the other day, and he said something like, "It's an astonishing thing to me, but in my observation true, that there is in a part of what we call the world — which certainly is, in the main, a good-natured, always-steadily-improving world — this curious propensity to run up a little score against, and as it were be even with, those who amuse and beguile us." Very interesting. Astounding that that was going on in 1869. But it's very confusing for actors because they don't quite know if they should be proud of their job or keep very quiet about it. The idea that you are slowly acquiring more and more skill, depth, daring, and all that kind of thing — that's an unforgivable thought to have; you just shut up and get on with it. Journalists love to hear actors say, "I just did the job for the money." "Yes! That's what we wanted to hear!" as they crow with delight. "We knew that was the only reason you ever did anything." And then, and only then, they forgive you, because you have no aspirations, just ambition and greed. That's human, that's unpretentious, the virtue of virtues in Britain. But to have a concept of your work as important or interesting — unforgivable. Don't dare to expect any respect for what you do.

The Audience

Spectacle has always been prized in the theatre. People have always loved it. But it is always in danger of overwhelming the theatrical experience. At present, most people who go to see plays on Broadway or in London go for the scenery and the decibels. I don't think they go to the theatre to be profoundly stirred anymore. When they are, it takes them by surprise and sometimes they don't like it. If they did like it, there'd be more of it. Supply and demand.

In the theatre, the audience is 50 percent of the experience. The theatre is the ultimate, original interactive experience. If people realized that, they might be rather more excited about it than when they go to the cinema, where they are absolutely passive and have no influence on the event whatever. There's this strange phenomenon that this performance will never be repeated; it can't be. Unfortunately, the bigger musicals that are completely controlled technologically do tend to be 100 percent the same; and the moment the theatre becomes totally repeatable night after night, then it ceases to be theatre. The all-important element of the theatre is this living interchange. As the great music hall comedian Max Wall used to say at the end of every performance, "Ladies and gentlemen, thank you very much. You have been half."

4
Martha Lavey

Martha Lavey has been artistic director of Chicago's award-winning Steppenwolf Theatre Company since 1995 and an ensemble member since 1993. Founded in 1976, Steppenwolf is one of America's longest lived and most celebrated theatre companies. She gave this interview in the spring of 2003.

Geography

In England, the centers of the film and theatre worlds are coincident in London; that makes a big difference. Here in Chicago, of course, our ensemble is affected on a daily basis by the fact that those two worlds are geographically dispersed.

Every single hiatus from his television work, John Mahoney comes screaming out of L.A. to work on a play. Some of the other, less well-known actors in the ensemble are there because they can piece together a living in a way that they can't here. Many would rather live here, but they can't.

The people who live here have to do something else as well. Commercial voice-over has been fairly strong here and has been the bread and butter for a lot of actors in this town, but now I hear them lamenting that even that work is going to known actors. Gary Sinise, for instance, last year took the job being the voice of Cadillac. In days of yore, that would have been some anonymous actor with a good voice. At the same time, reality television has usurped a lot of the work in made-for-TV movies so that the journeymen actors lost that work too. And they do less shooting here than they used to because a lot of film and series work got lost to Canada, which gives a tremendous tax incentive to filmmakers.

I don't know that it's possible to make a living working exclusively as a stage actor here.

Identity

Doing voice work is a different psychic investment than film. One's persona as an actor is not impinged upon by doing voice work. You go down to Leo Burnett in your jeans and you do the gig and you go home and you can be very clear that it's just a gig. Whereas, when you do a television show, for instance, your identity as an actor starts being represented in a way that may feel at odds with your stage life. I think about the actors I know who are on television shows. I went to college with David Schwimmer. What's the name of his character? Ross? Right. For millions of people, that's who David Schwimmer is. But he's actually a fantastic stage actor. And I think he's very torn by it.

John Malkovich is famous on the subject. He's constantly dishonoring the task of movie acting and moviemaking. But then, don't think he's going to give it up! He has a home in southern France, and he's a citizen of the world and hobnobs with really interesting people. The facile thing is to say that you shouldn't participate in it — that it is the Faustian bargain.

New York Acting

In New York, the contract is somewhat different as to what constitutes a good performance. It's very striking. Of course, I am utterly chauvinistic; I like Chicago acting a lot better than I like New York acting. To me, New York acting is extroverted in a way that just doesn't feel true. There is almost a presentational quality to the performance that serves the heightened ego of the audience because, if I'm winking at you while I am performing, then I am saying, "I'm not forgetting you. I'm doing this for you."

The other extreme is Malkovich, who is famous for performing with his back to the audience. And that comes out of a feeling that we have our life on stage; I am paying attention to you, my fellow actor, rather than to what's going on out there. Clearly that's also part of the allure of film. It constructs the voyeuristic circle much more reliably than the stage does. Film critics have written a lot about this — the idea that in watching a film, I can feel like I am overhearing these two people; I have access to what is private. Which is why I think film is so connected to sex and violence — things we hide from the public.

The Steppenwolf Style

The original Steppenwolf members will say that their ideals of acting were formed by film, and specifically the films of John Cassavetes. Remember, the late 1970s was a really fantastic period in American filmmaking; Hollywood was making movies for grownups with real acting. And that was what the founders here wanted to be able to do on stage — to achieve that level of daring and bravado and realism, and just take the gloves off. They felt that the only place they really saw that was on film and they wanted to do it in the room with the audience.

Their talent was translatable to Hollywood because what they strived for and achieved was truth in relationship. They weren't especially interested in being the kind of well-honed acting machine that graduate schools are putting out now, trained in dialect work and sword play. Their resource was point of view and passion and willingness to connect. And somehow that worked in Hollywood.

Sustaining an Ensemble

The people who started this theatre, who created its heartbeat, are still involved and keep us true to the original impulse. Gary Sinise, Jeff Perry, Terry Kinney — I talk to those guys daily. They are still passionate about the theatre, and they work here as artists and they help to sustain the legacy of the place. There is that amazing continuation.

The downside of their success, of course, is just having an ensemble of actors who have a lot of career alternatives makes it a lot harder to block out their time and to get them here.

I think it would be harder now to create an ensemble the way they did then. People have to be willing to close themselves off in a basement and not want to be anywhere else. It is very hard for young actors to commit to a company now. The enticements are so constant and ubiquitous. It seems to be harder for young people to say, "I'm going to be satisfied with the deep rewards of working collectively to build each other as artists."

Having our founders still so involved helps with that. When they come back, they're reminded of the value and the depth of the experience they had here, and they convey that to the younger members of the ensemble. Gary will say, "You know, Martha, lots of people can be film actors. There is no question that starting a theatre company will be the most distinct achievement of my life."

But I don't think another Steppenwolf is likely to happen here because Chicago has become a platform, a launching pad. The next Steppenwolf is going to happen somewhere no one is looking, out of the spotlight.

Envy

In theatre, at its best, we do the kind of art we want to do and we accept that this is the audience with whom we have contact, and the satisfaction becomes the work and the rapport with each other and the relationship with the audience. To me that has to be good enough; we have to give up that kind of frantic envy we feel because we're not reaching the larger audience that a movie can attract. One has to say to oneself — putting aside any covetousness about what I imagine the rewards of that other life are — "Do I like my life?" And for me, a life in the theatre is a really cool life. I wasn't born in this city, but I have become a part of this theatre community and this city in a way that is profoundly meaningful to me; it gives me a sense of place which I did not particularly have growing up. You are so tapped into a whole history; you feel yourself part of a theatre community and a legacy; it's fun to hang out at the proper bars afterwards — and all of that has much more allure to me than living among palm trees with a lot of dough.

But it's hard within the context of the value system that our culture propagates, which says you should really want fame, you should really want money. I feel like one of the luckiest people in the world because I have had a lot of contact with people who have fame and money, and I see what it costs them, and that makes it very clear that it's not for me. Some of my actor friends who started here are now in L.A. I ask them if they're happy and they'll say in a cynical sort of way, "Well, you know, Martha, we really like the weather."

A Particular Form of Torture

As a younger woman, when I was concentrating on acting, there was a very brief interval in there when I was starting to get calls from L.A. I went out for a couple of things and there was a certain amount of buzz — "young and pretty and talented" and so on. But it was right at that moment that I chose to start graduate school. So at that kind of teetery moment, when things might have fallen a certain way, I was looking the other way.

And here's what I missed: I remember a job I was out there for. The casting director was pulling for me, telling them, "She's a really good actress." It looked good for a while, but then I didn't get it. The feedback my agent got from the network was, "There's a glamour issue." So I kept trying to tease out what that meant, and eventually I got my agent to tell me: what that meant was that my breasts weren't large enough. So what I missed was that particular form of torture. Nobody is good enough there.

Beauty

If I film your face, either you have those goods — that set of features — or you don't. It's a kind of accident. And there are people whose beauty is amped up on camera; there is something about being under that kind of scrutiny that makes them come alive.

What matters on the stage is presence — how one fills a room — and there are those who become luminously beautiful by standards that Hollywood would reject outright. Something about that moment of being on the lit platform brings out whatever is best in them.

Acting and Gender Roles

There's an old saying, "An actress, more than a woman; an actor, less than a man." Well, I think that's really interesting, because socially that *is* part of the treatment. Being an actress empowers one with a certain kind of social license. I've gotten away with all kinds of stuff as a woman in a very sexist society on the basis of being an actress. By taking the stage, I demand that you look at me and listen to me. I'm standing on the lighted platform and it's my turn and just listen to me. And that translates to regular life, where I can get away with demanding presence in the room.

And the other part of the saying — "less than a man" — is about the fact that men, who routinely suck all the air out of the room, are never allowed to look like they are asking for it. It's just theirs. That's their territory. So when an actor puts himself in the position of consciously asking for your approbation or applause, that's not manly.

Realism

Television is one of our sources for cultural codes and behavior. It becomes a factor in shaping our understanding of what realistic acting is. I haven't owned a television in ten years, but when I walk into a hotel or health club and see something on television, I'm absolutely struck by the ghoulishly unnatural behavior I see. Even on news programs, there's this extremely exaggerated, slightly sexual teasing banter that goes on between anchors that is supposed to signal collegiality but that looks to me like really desperate behavior.

Malkovich says, famously, "The big fallacy is that the camera doesn't lie. That's what the camera is designed to do." The place where you can't lie is on stage. You can't edit a performance together.

Existential Truths

I've often thought that it would be fun to act in a serious role on film. All the stuff I've done has been a little lightweight. But it would be great to know that, "Okay, I am taking the gloves off, and I can do that because this is the last time I have to do it. I don't have to worry about whether I can recover from this." When I took Meisner classes, which are all about this in-the-moment truthfulness, it was much easier to access that core in an improvisation because it never had to be repeated. It is when one is thinking about having to return to that place tomorrow afternoon and again tomorrow night — that's really hard.

Sometimes when stage actors spend a lot of time in Hollywood, they lose the do-or-die quality of stage. Most obviously, working on stage, you can't look at any performance as if it's another take and you'll get it later if you don't get it now. On stage, it has to really matter every single time. Psychically, that is a very difficult investment to make. There has to be a real drive to do that. Our actors will be very honest and say to me, "You know what, Martha? I don't want to be on the stage anymore. I'm too tired. I did it once. But it's too hard."

So my respect for stage actors has grown tremendously in the last years as I get older. I'm forty-five now, and when I was younger, theatre acting just seemed fantastic; all that energy, all that intensity. But I didn't understand that acting would become perilous over time, because the technical resources one needs on stage — physical strength, vocal strength, memory, emotional candor — are all things that nature takes away from us as we get older. So to keep putting it out there just seems like an incredible act of courage to me now.

And accompanying that are the difficulties of the career. Most people in society at large can look at their career and the trajectory is basically on an upward incline. An actor doesn't have that assurance at all.

And to put oneself in that place existentially seems to me terribly brave. I think about the actual act of going on stage. What is that? It's a very weird, highly ritualized thing. We show up at the theatre at the same time. One's moves in a play are almost identical and to the clock every night.

And then it's over. It requires a willingness to come into very close contact with one's mortality and with the Sisyphean task of life — to get close to the futility of life, but also to find underneath what is valuable. There is not some big, conquering moment; the job is just somehow to find joy or radiance in the fact that, yep, every single day it's the same old thing.

With film, there is at least an accumulated body of work — a trail left behind one, a visible legacy. Whereas, of a stage performance, all we can do is say, "Do you remember that?" We can only tell each other about the production of *Balm in Gilead* that we saw. And actually, I cherish that kind of legacy. I don't have to look at the hard evidence and say, "Well, actually that performance wasn't so great," or "Oh, I was so young!" Whatever it was that was the core of our experience, the thing that made it luminous and beautiful, time can't take away when it is our shared memory.

5
Frank Rich

Frank Rich, a columnist and associate editor for the New York Times, *was chief drama critic for the paper from 1980 to 1993. This telephone interview was conducted in the spring of 2000.*

It's Nothing New

If you look at the history of the commercial theatre, if you literally chart Broadway openings as a reliable barometer of the commercial theatre, you'll find that, in the '20s, there were nearly three hundred productions a season. That number fell in the late '20s, and for one concrete reason: *The Jazz Singer.* From the late '20s to the late '40s, the number of Broadway productions continued to fall to an average of around eighty plays or so. The next big downturn Broadway took was in the late '40s, with the rise of television, and that brought Broadway to the state it's in now, when there will be thirty to forty plays a season, maximum. Talking pictures and then television cut into Broadway theatre — and into theatre as a centerpiece of American culture — and theatre has never recovered, becoming over this period a very secondary part of American culture. In the '30s and '40s, Broadway would lead *Variety*; now it's often relegated to a few pages near the back. Its prominence in general interest publications has similarly declined.

As far as stars go, it's long been the case that actors make their names in the theatre and then immediately leave and go to Hollywood. Clark Gable was in *Machinal* on Broadway in the late '20s; Jack Barrymore went to Hollywood after his triumphs on stage in the same period. Audrey Hepburn was discovered in the theatre, then came back only once or twice. Dustin Hoffman, whose career began Off-Broadway in the '60s, came back to do *Death of a Salesman* and *Merchant of Venice* on Broadway in the '80s. But these stars didn't give up their day jobs in Hollywood. It's no different now. Calista Flockhart, to take one recent example, was a very good Off-Broadway actress. Then, in the early '90s, she was discovered and went west, almost never to return.

There's nothing new about any of this. Nothing has changed except the names. Stars come back only for fun or if their careers are in trouble in

Hollywood. So Kelsey Grammer, who began in the theatre in the '80s in New York, comes back as a lark to do *Macbeth* for a very limited run. If Nicole Kidman does theatre, she's only going to do it for three months and then will leave. Hollywood stars who do theatre for extended runs are people whose careers are in trouble. You know if Christian Slater goes into *Side Man*, it's because he just got out of drug rehab.

Corporate Money in Theatre

Periodically, movie companies get interested in investing in plays and producing them, but that's also an old pattern. Go back to the '50s and the '70s, and even earlier, and you're going to find 20th Century Fox, Paramount, and other Hollywood people involved in Broadway producing. Generally what happens is that the movie companies get burned and then they leave.

What *is* a new trend in the commercial theatre is that big corporations have supplanted the individual producer. This was brought home recently by the deaths of David Merrick and Alex Cohen. Big corporations are trying to market Broadway shows as if they were Hollywood products or record industry products. That never happened before because no one could afford to do it. Television advertising for the theatres didn't begin in earnest until the '70s, and even then it was just for a few musicals, since no one else could afford it. So you have these companies like Disney, the now-defunct Livent, and SFX [later absorbed by Clear Channel, probably the biggest and most powerful of all of them], and they're trying to bring those merchandizing techniques to gaudy musicals, whether it be *Footloose* or *Fosse* or *The Lion King* or *Jesus Christ Superstar*. They're trying, but the fact is that some may eventually get out of the business because it doesn't really pay, the expenses and risks are so high.

The Audience

Many playwrights feel that television, in particular, over the last generation has fractured attention spans, and this is reflected in the fact that many contemporary plays are written in a lot of short takes. I don't know it for a fact, but this may have less to do with changes in the audience than with the effect of television on the artists themselves. *Death of a Salesman*, Bob Falls' production, was three hours long, and people had no problem with it. Similarly, to my amazement, there does seem to be an audience for *Moon for the Misbegotten*, and it's not that Cherry Jones and Gabriel Byrne are such huge stars — they're not. People want to see that play. So, if it's good, audiences have the attention span. Indeed, a lot of people who look at the culture point out that there's a huge market for long books — fiction and contemporary biography. Look at the bestseller list: there are a lot of books that are long, and that sell, and that people apparently read. It's not that everyone is just reading bite-size fiction.

Broadway Economics

You can't have more than three or four straight plays on Broadway at a time, no matter what they are. That has more to do with the demographics of

New York and the economics of producing than with any of the cultural issues. Broadway plays are hugely expensive to produce; therefore ticket prices have gone higher and higher, and they've priced out of the market virtually everyone except tourists. And so where once upon a time 70 percent of the Broadway audiences were New York based, now it's something like 30 percent. And if people are paying seventy dollars and up for a ticket, they don't want straight plays. There's a real ceiling on that audience, but it has nothing to do with attention spans or the rise of TV; it has to do with the marketplace. If tourists are paying that kind of money, they want to see spectacle; they want to see where their money went. If you're paying ninety dollars, you don't want to see three people talking about nuclear physics. So, in a way, it's become more like a theme park or like Vegas. You wouldn't go to Vegas to see *Copenhagen*, and it's pretty much the same in New York. But this has been true for years. It's just gotten worse and worse as costs have gone up.

And yes, the largest mass is going to want the lowest common denominator stuff, but that was true two hundred years ago or seventy years ago. *Tobacco Road* was a bigger hit than *Strange Interlude*. What does that prove? There is always an elite audience for intellectual fare, and I don't think the proportional size of that audience has changed that much. That kind of audience has been driven out of the Broadway marketplace not because it's shrinking so much as because tickets are so expensive. There's still a small percentage that wants to go to plays and can afford to, but, according to *Variety*, in any given week in recent years, the entire gross of straight plays on Broadway rarely totals more than 15 percent of the total; the other 85 or 90 percent of it is musicals. The ratio of serious theatre to disposable entertainment was no different in the '20s. Ninety percent of it was crap of some sort, if not necessarily musicals back then, and 90 percent of it is completely forgotten now. The disposable plays then were the equivalent of *Party of Five* or *Three's Company* today. Theatre then had a much more central role because mass electronic media hadn't been developed. What's gone now is the stuff that TV and movies do better. Why go see the silly sex comedy on Broadway — and that's now an extinct form — when you can watch it any night on Fox, probably done better and more conveniently and certainly cheaper.

Writers

The economics make it very hard to do a new play now, and one concomitant aspect of it is that playwrights leave the theatre because there's no work for them. If you go and look at the house writers of *ER*, *Law & Order*, or *The West Wing*, you're going to find a Who's Who of Off-Broadway playwrights of the last twenty years — writers who had no chance of getting a play on Broadway, which means that they had no chance of making a living wage, and so they fled. And directors too. Peter Parnell, to take one example of a writer, was a wonderful playwright and had a number of plays produced at Playwrights' Horizon in the '80s, some of them shown on *American Playhouse* on PBS.

Now he's working for *The West Wing* because there's no room for him to make a living in theatre.

Those economics are filtering into the nonprofit movement: they need to do commercial stuff to pay their bills because they can't make it on ticket sales. And while there are theatres that don't succumb to that — the Goodman would be a handy example — more common is the Alliance Theatre in Atlanta getting involved with Disney in *Aida*. It's the same need for income that drives nonprofit companies to do endless revivals of old favorites, including musicals.

Liveness

There will always be a hunger for live entertainment. Let's take it out of the realm of theatre. Look at professional sports. Why do people go and pay exorbitant amounts of money to go to NFL games or NBA games when you can not only see them on television, you can actually see them *better* on television? Why do people go to rock concerts when you could just buy the record? This is one reason the theater is not extinct and never will be. But it is not a major part of the cultural firmament in America right now, and it hasn't been since the '50s.

6
Peter Parnell

American playwright Peter Parnell is the author of the stage version of The Cider House Rules — Parts I & II, *adapted from the novel by John Irving;* QED; *and* Romance Language. *He has worked in Hollywood, including as writer and producer for the television series* The Guardian, *and as writer, executive story editor, and co-producer of* The West Wing. *He was in L.A. working on* The West Wing *at the time of this interview in the spring of 2000.*

Subsidizing a Career

There has been a greater receptivity to playwrights writing for television in the last few years. Because of cable and the number of new channels, television is trying to develop a new identity for itself and find a new audience by being slightly more experimental, slightly edgier, you know. And to do that, both the networks and cable are looking to writers who have a bit more of a skewed vision, which includes playwrights. Playwriting tends to be fresher because the risk is all about doing the work. It's not about making money; it never has been as a playwright. Your voice is the main thing that you go with. So television has become more receptive to playwrights now than it was fifteen to twenty years ago.

I know a number of playwrights who are writing for TV, as well as a number of playwrights who are writing movies. I think in this day and age you need to be able to write many different things, and there's nothing wrong with that. It doesn't change the fact that if you love to write plays, you will continue to write plays.

Geography

To write a weekly series, you generally do have to live in Los Angeles. To create a series, no, you don't; to write a pilot, obviously, you don't. But if you are going to work with a company of actors who are producing week after week in Hollywood, that's where you have to be. If you are writing a show which is shot in New York, then you write it in New York, or you travel there for the production of your episode. Canada has a lot of production as well.

My partner and I live in New York. I don't think I would pick up stakes and move here to L.A. I can't really envision that. But the work I'm doing here is quite rewarding. The scripts are really smart and I like the pace of it. And I love the ensemble. It's like having a rep company that's there for you, in a way. I find that quite exciting. So the struggle I have right now is that I want to be here because I want to work on this show, but that means I'm commuting.

The Talent Drain

Where I do think Hollywood is a big problem for playwrights is with actors. The economics now are such that very often producers want to have that actor who they think will sell tickets. And there's certainly nothing wrong with somebody who's a wonderful movie actor doing a play, if you can get him or her to do it. But agents often don't want actors to be in plays. Actors who need to make money — and it's very hard to make money in the theatre for everybody — don't want to do plays. Actors have to be seduced into doing a play. It's a very big deal to get an actor to say, on his or her hiatus or between movies, "Yes, I will come and do this play."

Most of the actors that I knew when I was starting out in New York as a playwright are now living in Hollywood acting in television and movies. Occasionally, the *New York Times* will write a big article when five stars decide to do Broadway or Off-Broadway plays for a season, saying, "The actors are coming back!" Well, they have no idea what underlies that — the handholding, the arm-twisting, the agents lying that actors are not available because they don't want their clients to do plays.

And it's a problem with directors because, of course, directors can also make more money directing television and movies. After a director has done several plays on Broadway or Off-Broadway, he or she will invariably want to supplement the theatre work by learning how to work on television and will come out here to trail on a show or trail on a show in New York. And as you get older, of course, economics become more of a factor — you know, you want to be able to live a little better. So the older directors tend to leave the theatre and work primarily in film and in television.

I am not saying that this is necessarily bad. It's good that there's a place for directors to direct. But that drain does happen, and it is bad for the theatre when talented directors totally stop doing plays.

Critics

A New York critic who supported my work and who intended to review a play of mine couldn't make it at the last moment. So the editorial board sent a critic who hadn't liked the last number of plays I had done. The opening paragraph in that critic's review attacked the last three plays I had written before reviewing the play that he had just seen. Now, if that doesn't get a playwright thinking, "Why am I writing a play for this city?" I don't know what does. When the New York critics say "no" to a play, it's very hard for the playwright to turn around and write another play, but that's just the name of the game. You have to be very strong to do it. But you do it.

Hit or Miss

Brian Clark, the British playwright who wrote *Who's Life Is it Anyway?*, once made the comment in the *New York Times* that a healthy theatre is a theatre in which a mediocre play can run for a while. I totally agree with that. When you have a hit-or-miss mentality, you are in trouble, because that means that every new play has to be a sensation, has to totally capture the moment, has to epitomize something in order for people to see it. On Broadway, the economics of sixty-five dollars a ticket has forced that to happen. My ideal would be to have a Broadway that produced many more straight plays than are now running. In a better world, you could have mediocre plays that would run because a certain star is in them or because they are a vehicle for a social idea that's interesting.

A Terrible Profession

Playwriting has always been a terrible profession. Robert Anderson, who wrote *Tea and Sympathy*, said famously years ago, "You can make a killing on Broadway. You just can't make a living there." That's true, and it becomes even truer as the number of straight plays produced on Broadway becomes fewer. Very often writers have to defer royalties in order for a Broadway play to run. The average run for an Off-Broadway not-for-profit play is six weeks, which is not going to bring a playwright a lot of money.

What we're missing now are commercial producers for the serious plays of established playwrights. Broadway doesn't produce straight plays anymore, really, except maybe one or two a year, and a lot of them are British imports. So all the writers who could be writing on Broadway have moved to Off-Broadway, even including the midlife playwrights. The not-for-profit Off-Broadway theatres have moved into the role of producing the work of our premier, top-notch, established playwrights — from Wendy Wasserstein and Chris Durang to Pete Gurney and Arthur Kopit. They are all being produced by the not-for-profits, at least initially.

And since the not-for-profits have limited real estate, limited resources, and limited money, the opportunities Off-Broadway have shrunk for new playwrights, who are now competing for the same pool of not-for-profit theatres: a twenty-five-year-old playwright is competing for the same slot in a theatre as Pete Gurney. There are lots of ways that younger playwrights, developing playwrights, can get their work heard and read. We have a mechanism in place to have young playwrights go to training camps like the O'Neill playwright's conference or other places where you can hear your work done. There are kind of laboratories for that. But to get fully produced as a new playwright is much harder.

And at the same time, the middle playwrights aren't being nurtured enough to develop their vision because they are totally subject to all of those problems in New York that prevent you from developing as a writer. The future of their plays depends largely on economics and the critical establishment in New York; their plays either will have a future life or not based on a good review or a large marketing campaign. It's very hard to have much of a run.

And if you start your play in New York and it doesn't do well there — if it doesn't have a long run — it will also not be picked up by the regional theatres, it won't be produced over and over again, and you will not be able to earn a living. Playwrights who in the past would start in New York now try very hard to get their plays done regionally before a New York production so they can really work on them, because New York is such a very tough market.

The Fabulous Invalid

Of course, the theatre has always thought that it was dying. George S. Kaufman and Moss Hart wrote a Broadway play in the '40s called *The Fabulous Invalid*. The set is an old, torn-down Broadway theatre and it's supposed to be the last night of the use of the space, and they play out satires of scenes of previous great Broadway plays. It's a very angry piece. It's basically saying that the theatre is imperiled, but it's also ultimately saying that the theatre has always thought that it is in peril. The theatre is just a terrible place, but it is a wonderful place, too, you know; it's just filled with terrible and great things.

7

Richard Monette

Since 1994, Richard Monette has served as the artistic director of the Stratford Festival in Ontario, Canada, where he has also played more than forty roles. The festival is one of the few resident repertory companies in North America, currently employing more than 140 actors, some of whom have been with the company for decades. Monette has performed throughout Canada, Britain, and the United States, including in plays on Broadway and in the West End. He has more than thirty film and television credits, including as director of two film adaptations of Shakespeare comedies. This interview was conducted in the summer of 2004.

Training Shakespearean Actors

Many young actors hope to work in film or television and are not daring — or even yearning — to try classical theatre. But there are always actors who want to do Shakespeare, and those are the people you want in your company. So you ask, "What do you want to do? Do you want to make a lot of money? Do you want a series and to be famous? Or do you want to tackle the great roles?" There will always be a finite number of people who want to do this kind of work. It's a vocation.

But even those young actors who have the vocation really don't do enough Shakespeare because very few schools require it. If you're doing contemporary drama, it doesn't equip you to do Shakespeare; whereas if you can do Shakespeare, you can do anything else. That's why we established our conservatory for classical training. It was self-serving because the young actors were coming here from theatre school having done one Shakespeare in three years, which meant we had to train them as we were directing, and there's simply not enough time.

Ours is a one-year program: For seventeen weeks the actors are paid an equity wage to study; then they are guaranteed a nine-month season. It is specifically about classical work. We have a thousand applications a year. We go through Canada from coast to coast, and to Chicago because we have an association there. We audition five hundred; we choose twelve. Five classes have now gone through the program, and the dividends have been huge: we now have gotten about seven leading players out of this. So something we're doing is right for classical work.

Spear-Carrying

The young people who come into the company as spear carriers learn that everybody's there to put up a play, and whether you speak one line or three thousand lines, it's all part of the orchestra, it's all feeding in. More importantly, you listen to William Hutt, who's been speaking this verse for fifty years. You learn by osmosis. You're onstage with these great actors for nine months and you absorb how Shakespeare is spoken.

That's how I learned. I was holding a spear in *Henry IV, Parts One and Two* when Douglas Rain was doing it in '65, '66. And when I got to do my Henry IV, I remembered every single line reading he did, from which I was able to take, imitate, and discard.

Life in Repertory

Repertory theatre is a dying art, which is too bad. In a repertory company — especially at this remove from the city — you can really concentrate on the work and all the life of the work that can be brought out. On the other hand, no life comes in from outside. It is hard if you're young: where do you party? But you can't have everything. This is one of the few theatres you can work in full time and actually buy a house, raise children, have a life.

Still, there comes a point when the star actors have done their Henry IVs and their Richard IIIs and their Hamlets, and now what do they do? Some of them feel they're going to atrophy here, so they leave. As a result, there's a missing generation in our company — my generation — that went to television. But my answer to that is you never atrophy if you're doing Shakespeare. If you want to explore the human condition, you're not going to do it on television.

One of my current sadnesses is that actors who've been here since very nearly the first season are now going to retire. Our company will change into a much younger company because our oldest generation is leaving. So one of the reasons I started the conservatory is to find young actors who will have the same dedication as those older actors who grew up in a world where the theatre was a profession.

Lyricism

Though I have not seen very good Shakespeare in America — and I've seen a great deal of it — I believe that American actors ought to be the best; I really don't know why they aren't. They have an immediacy; they have a fearlessness; they are adventurous when they tackle a new work. That energy just has to be harnessed.

But one of the things that we don't have anywhere in the world is an appetite for lyricism. That's what I think is missing in most Shakespeare performance. Brian Bedford, William Hutt, Domini Blythe, Seanna McKenna — they can all do this. But ask someone twenty- or thirty-something to give you a long lyric line and it's like you're asking them to fly to the moon. They are reductive.

They don't believe in it. And you can't do Shakespeare unless you believe in it. You have to have something in yourself that wants to articulate that place in your soul, that yearning, that desire, that mystery.

Film Acting

Paul Newman and Joanne Woodward came to see Chris Plummer in *Lear*. They came back to my office at the interval and the first words out of Mr. Paul Newman were, "This makes me feel so inadequate." Now this man is arguably one of the two or three greatest living film actors. What he was responding to was not only Chris's technique but the play.

Acting for film and television is very different from on stage. You get a genius like Marlon Brando who apparently read his lines in *Apocalypse Now* off cards, yet it's an astonishing performance.

Naturalism

People think film is naturalistic. But in a film, a character might be speaking and all you see is her mouth. That's something that you can't optically do in life; it's not "natural." I can't see your mouth that close. Then you'll see a shot from sixty feet away; then there's whispering coming out in Dolby sound. What could be less natural? There's a misperception of what natural is.

Of course, art is never natural. Naturalism is an anathema to Shakespeare. Don't come on picking your nose; it has nothing to do with that. But it is real. In a theatre, you're in a room with a finite space, large or small. You're talking to another actor and you're talking to a real group of people. That's what people respond to: real people talking in a real space to real people. That is in fact what the theatre is about.

Shakespeare on Film

I think anything that makes Shakespeare available to a large audience is good. There are countries where you cannot see live Shakespeare. Those audiences can see Shakespeare only on film. And if some young people are turned on to Shakespeare because they see a Guns N' Roses version of *Romeo and Juliet*, like what Baz Luhrman did with DiCaprio, or they see Zefferelli's version, which I think is so beautiful, then that's great. You may not get the whole story or all the verse, but it's a primer.

When I was very young, I saw Laurence Olivier's *Richard III* on film and it was a revelation to me. I had no idea it would be that accessible, that funny, that theatrical. So it's all to the good. Whatever you do to a Shakespeare play, the play will live on.

The TV Generation Audience

Tyrone Guthrie said, "The only great theatre you see is when you're very young." My belief is that if they're brought here as children, the seed is planted. Then they have boyfriends, girlfriends, sex, dances, drugs, rock and roll; then they get married; then they save for the car, the house, the children;

and *then* they come back. But unless they're introduced when they're young, they will not come back.

That is why I started the Family Experience program, which provides cheaper tickets for children. We worried, though, that this generation — brought up on television, computers, all of that — wouldn't sit through a play. But it turns out they do. I was actually going to cut out the program. Apparently I get a lot of flack critically — though I haven't read a review in eight years — for doing things like the *Hunchback* and *Three Musketeers* and *Scarlet Pimpernel*. So I said, "Well fine, if the Board doesn't like it, nobody likes it, then we'll cut it." But then our staff announced that sales for the Family Experience are going through the roof. And I think that's because storytelling is older than the world's oldest profession, and even today's children still respond to it. It's a very social sharing, and I think that's really healthy. I don't make theatre to do therapy, but I do believe that to be true.

Shakespeare Now

When I began this job nine years ago in 1993, attendance was at 446,000; last year it was 608,000. The audiences are growing, not shrinking — at least from this theatre's point of view. So that's pretty encouraging.

We recently surveyed our audience in our newly built Studio Theatre and found out that nearly 85 percent were either university graduates or had postgrad degrees. So although we're labeled populist by the press because we do the musicals and the family shows, we will now be labeled elitists!

Most of the people who come here are empty-nesters. Now they're fifty, they're established, they're looking around spiritually. I think this kind of work appeals mostly to people who are not burdened by the everyday problems of life. It's a luxury in some sense. Of course, some people just come for the afternoon to see a musical and have a picnic. But mostly they come for Shakespeare. They want these texts; they want to see this kind of work. I also think there's something about our theatre itself. Our thrust stage is mythic; it's the closest thing to Epidauras. It evokes something from the audience because of its shape. It's not a movie screen; it's not a proscenium arch. There's something very ancient about it.

I don't want to sound pretentious here, but local religious leaders write me from time to time, "Our parishioners come from out of town and they say how important it is to them to come here because of their spiritual growth." Well, no one is more irreligious in a sense than Shakespeare. But people come because they need the spiritual nourishment. So rather than saying Shakespeare's threatened, I think he's going to be more and more valued because we don't have many options anymore. Going to a dance bar is not going to cut it. A bad movie is not going to cut it. People don't commune in churches as much as they used to. People don't believe in what churches are saying. But Shakespeare is telling a truth you believe in.

If you bring a young woman to see *Lear*, she will view the play with great sympathy toward Cordelia. When she returns at the age of sixty to see *Lear*, the story will be different for her. Our audiences want to see sides; they want that mythic quality. Otherwise, you do *Lear* and all you get is a documentary about some old man getting Alzheimer's. The human condition expressed in *Lear* is bigger than that. And that, of course, is Shakespeare's genius. As we go on in life we try to catch up to him because the stories, the characterizations, the verse, the insights are always what you're going through, always what you need.

The son of our executive director is nine years old, and he said two weeks ago to his father, "Whenever I see a Shakespeare play, I'm always sad even when it's funny." He stopped me dead in my mental tracks. He's a very kind of sporty kid; he's not a Hamlet, he's not reflective. So I thought about this a lot and I came to this conclusion, rightly or wrongly: that because the iambic pentameter follows the human heartbeat, and because the iambic line is long, and because Shakespeare's stories take such a journey, the plays reach you on a level that is primal. In Shakespeare, rhythm is everything: how you bring people on, how you bring them off, how they speak. And that's one of the many reasons why audiences respond to him. The plays are so in tune with our rhythm that it makes everything — as the kid might have said if he could — elegiac. No matter how beautiful a sunset may be, you're always sad somewhere inside. The ending of a day, the ending of beauty. It's what John Ruskin called oceanic feelings: there is something profoundly affecting in each play's beauty and rhythm.

People wring their hands: Shakespeare's dying, theatre's dying, everybody's watching television, nobody's reading. I don't agree because I think human beings — whatever their many shortcomings — have a life force that Shakespeare articulates. A character like Falstaff ingests life; he just eats it like Mars eating his children. Or Hamlet, who is so complex, so sad, and yet he brings out the life of the audience. I believe that Shakespeare writes from such truth, originality, and life force — even when it's as cynical as *Troilus and Cressida* — that it pushes through to an audience. I know I sound like a Moony, but I really believe that. I believe that he punctures into life.

8
Julie Taymor

Julie Taymor is a director of theatre, film, and opera. Widely known for her direction and design of the acclaimed Broadway production of The Lion King, *she also directed the film* Titus, *based on Shakespeare's play* Titus Andronicus, *starring Anthony Hopkins and Jessica Lange, and directed the film* Frida, *starring Salma Hayek and Alfred Molina. This interview was given in early 2004.*

The Elements of Theatre

Film fills in the imagery for you more than theatre does. In the theatre, a man and a woman can be alone on an empty stage talking and it is their words that provide the imagery, which is seen by the audience in their imaginations but not literally on stage. In film, though the imagery can be abstract and fantastic, it is usually completed for you.

Interestingly, theatre audiences can fill in more blanks because they have seen so much TV and film. They don't need to see a savannah fully represented on the stage because they know what a savannah looks like already. Even children have seen so much that you can give them less and they will understand the allusions. It is a pleasure of the contemporary theatre that you can use a kind of shorthand because the audience is becoming more visually experienced, more visually literate.

In *The Lion King,* I hoped the audience would be moved by the story and the songs, of course, but I hoped equally that they would be emotionally moved by the *art* of the theatrical storytelling. There can be a spiritual thrill in watching a performer manipulate a puppet — a thrill that goes back to the origins of theatre. The animation of the inanimate, the breathing of life into an object — that was the role of the shaman. The shadows played on a cave wall were in fact the origins of a theatrical experience. Magic is in the ability of the human being to imagine. In *The Lion King,* the audience sees grass growing in the savannah. The fact that the grass is actually planted on platters that sit on top of the dancers' heads can just make the experience all the more exciting.

I often use the sun as an example when I talk about the choices we made in *The Lion King*. The actual object is made of strips of saffron silk that rest on the floor in a heap and then get pulled up by strings. There's no doubt that I could have done a perfect projection of a sunrise in the theatre, but that approach is best suited to film and television. I wanted to do what the theatre does best, which is to put an object in front of you that you know is insubstantial — just a piece of fabric hanging from a stick — and, as it is raised, you see the sun rise. That is thrilling — the sensation of life being breathed into an object by the addition of human imagination.

By contrast, film is literal. In a film, you would show the grass growing out of the earth; you would show an actual sunrise. Of course, you don't have to stay always within that kind of literal reality, even in film. In *Frida*, for example, the figure of Death sang and spoke with Frida. By bringing the paintings to life, I was able to represent both her inner and her outer reality. One can certainly create an expressionistic or surreal style in film, but it isn't done as frequently. Whereas that inner reality is addressed all the time in theatre: the action may suddenly dissolve into a dream sequence or a ghost will appear. And that, to me, is where theatre potentially surpasses film, because it is better equipped to deal in the abstract, in layers of imagery and symbolism.

That doesn't mean that the theatre is less accessible. To the contrary, children are much more sophisticated than adults at being able to recognize reality in the abstract. They will look at white silk coming out of the character's eyes and they'll see tears. They don't need to translate it; they get it right away. That's why they can make believe with very little. Or they used to be able to. Now, computers are probably destroying that ability and making us a very literal and simplistic-minded people.

The tactile nature of theatre is also very important. You can see the ripples of silk in the sun. When a hyena comes down the aisle, you are brushed by it. I think people need those visceral experiences. There are those who say TV and film are going to wipe out live theatre. I don't think so. Is cyber sex ever going to replace sex? Why do people like boxing so much? Boxing is an ancient form of organized violence, and an art, if you like it; but the essence of it is the blood and sweat flying, the pure finesse of the athlete, and that essential human impulse: "Get him, get him, till you win." Those things are so human, they don't seem to me to be going anywhere. Why else are all those people attending the live event of boxing when they could simply watch it on TV?

When you go to a movie theatre, you are not paying attention to your neighbor in the next seat. You are trying to be anonymous; there is no sense of the liveness of the event, so the experience is easily transferable to your home system. And though the premiere of a movie is an event because of all the glitz that surrounds it, it's not the nature of film itself.

Theatre is about creating a sense of awe in a space, creating something that is larger than the banal. Sitting together with other people in a space where something is happening that has a certain kind of danger to it because it can fail — like the circus — that experience has something in common with the experience of being in a church or temple or mosque. We call those sacred spaces because a spiritual aspect of your being is being tapped, and I think that can happen when people go to live theatre as well.

Point of View

A theatre audience gets to choose what to look at. For instance, at *The Lion King*, you could be watching one of the puppeteer-actors manipulate the puppet, or you could just focus on the puppet and forget that there are three people manipulating it. In contrast, a film director, with his or her D.P. [Director of Photography] chooses exactly the point of view the audience will see. No matter where you are sitting, you are going to get essentially the same picture. That is one of the reasons you have to be very visually precise in film.

Well, you don't *have* to be — just look at all the crappy movies out there. Many filmmakers don't seem to give a damn about the potential power of the camera. But that's largely because of television, which has affected film in a very negative way. For one thing, television has spoiled us with close-ups. Because it's small, TV relies on the close-up to convey the actor's facial expressions and language. But using a close-up doesn't necessarily get you any deeper into the emotions of the character; it's just an easy shorthand. Sticking a camera in the face of someone who's crying doesn't necessarily convey sadness. Sadness can be also conveyed by framing the actor as a small creature in a vast empty room; that can be just as expressive. You can't do that with TV. If you pull your camera far enough away to see a whole set, the image of the actor is too small on the television screen. All of these techniques — close-up, long shot, high angle or low angle, dark or light — should be part of your vocabulary to tell the story. But television tends to limit that vocabulary.

Hear and See

In France, they call theatre "le spectacle." We think, and our critics think, that spectacle is empty, like the special effects in the movies. But theatre is comprised of visual imagery as much as language. The Greeks staged their plays with stylized masked actors instead of the naturalism of a naked face. A play on the page is not theatre. Shakespeare has been edited over and over again by the actors who put on his plays. Theatre is not a script of words; it's what one puts on stage. That doesn't mean you can't get something out of reading great plays, but even Shakespeare comes alive when staged.

And you can't just get up there in your jeans, either; Shakespeare's poetic language demands a poetic visual language as well. In filming *Titus*, I wanted a visual world that balanced the world of the language. For instance, in the opening sequences, I tried to create the feeling that the child, Lucius, was falling through an *Alice in Wonderland* hole of time. And that collision of three different historical periods as the setting for the film in fact follows

Shakespeare's own model — he mixed up Greek mythology, Virgil, Roman, and Elizabethan history with his own Christian morality.

More often, of course, it is theatre, rather than film, that retells familiar texts. Theatre can be as much about the art of interpreting a story as it is about the story itself. When you go to see your sixth *Henry IV*, as I just did, you can still get something out of it because some element in the production is new. People have been telling the stories represented in Kabuki theatre or the *Mahabharata* for centuries. The experience of seeing those stories in the theatre becomes about the interpretation: Did this actor's performance have more edge? What did he emphasize? How was the quality of the singing? Was the orchestra up to it? Those are the things you go for — the "art" of the theatre.

Writers

Rap music and hip hop have enlivened the appreciation and power of language among young people. The creative organization of language, slang, made-up words, the way words are edited and put together — it may not be "proper English-speak," but that's its very power. Young people actually have tremendous appreciation for language.

I think there are always ebbs and flows in writing, and there are always good plays and bad plays. In Shakespeare's time, all the dramatic writers were writing for the theatre. Now you have many good dramatic writers who have moved on to other media in order to make a living. It's as simple as that. If you write for television or you write for film, you can make a living. Trying to make a living as a writer in the theatre is a dicey proposition.

Musical Drama

In my Shakespeare productions there is always music. Shakespeare loved music. I wouldn't say that every play requires it, but music is an incredibly powerful tool for conveying emotional states and controlling energy and pacing.

I actually think opera, conceptually, is the quintessence of theatre. It is verbal, musical, and spectacle on three equal planes. Unfortunately, opera has a hurdle to get over, which is that younger people aren't attending in throngs. It's a shame that opera is not attracting young audiences because it is potentially the freest, wildest, and most grand of all mediums. It has tremendous potential to use language in interesting ways — though, of course, a lot of librettos don't exploit that potential — and it can be visually spectacular, and then it's stylized in the sense that you are singing your inner thoughts in the arias.

Musicals have that same potential, but it's hard to find the actors — the triple threats — who can sing and dance and act equally well. If you do a musical like *Chicago* on film, it's easier to pull off because you can enhance the weak singing. And if you're dealing with a movie star, the expectations are not as high: "Ohmigod, she can sing!" But one of the hazards of minimizing the weak dancing or singing is the overuse of cutting. If you look at those old

Gene Kelly films, he just danced and the cameras rolled. Very little intercutting of the choreography. If you've got that kind of talent, then don't cut the hell out of it.

The Abuses of Editing

There's too much editing in film in general. Too much cutting. People attribute it to MTV, but it began before that. People have grown up with it; it's a vocabulary. But there are filmmakers out there who just roll the camera and let a person talk and that can still work too.

We could have a long discussion about spoiled film directors. Directors think they can fix anything in the cutting room. I don't believe that. I believe that the script has to work from the beginning. And if you say you are going to do a two-hour film, don't shoot five hours of material. I haven't had that luxury, of course. I've done only two features, but almost everything I shot is in *Frida* and *Titus*. If it wasn't essential, then I didn't shoot it.

I actually think that limitations like that can push creativity. For instance, in *Frida*, we didn't have the money to shoot in Paris or New York, so we created the montage sequences instead, and I think they really added something. If I'd had the money to shoot New York, the result probably would have been lousy. I'm never one to be frightened of limitations. So often in the theatre — and film too — the limitations can inspire a really creative, beautiful solution.

Of course, I do enjoy the process of editing film, but where it gets very difficult is when you have producer-distributors who don't see eye-to-eye with you — who want more cuts and who do test screenings and all that. It all depends on who you decide to go to bed with. If you want to do a big budget movie — anything over twelve or fifteen million dollars — then you are at the mercy of whoever's giving you the money. That's true in theatre too, but there is generally more respect for the artists in theatre; the business people don't step in as much. It would be very difficult for a theatrical producer to come in and say, "I'm going to direct that actor differently." But in film now, especially with the advent of video and video editing, many producers think that they can show you what they want by recutting your film — you know, Bertolluci being cut by Harvey Weinstein. You read about that and you just want to run for the hills. It's horrific. Awful. You have to avoid that somehow if you want to be a filmmaker. Since I'm also in theatre, I have more choices. If I were just working in the film industry, I'd slit my throat.

The Demands of Film

I turn down a lot of film scripts because they are just not interesting enough to justify the investment of time. You have to spend a minimum of two years of your life on a film. By contrast, as a theatre director, you could say in January, "I will do such-and-such play in the spring." It would be very hard to do that with film. First, there's preproduction. Then shooting, which is the shortest amount of time. I spent four months shooting *Titus*, nine or ten weeks shooting *Frida*. Then you are in postproduction for a year and a half. And then you have to do all this hideous press. That is a much bigger part of film because the film is going all over the world. In theatre, if your play is in New York, you are not going to do press in Venice. But in film, as a director or as a lead actor, the press is unbelievably demanding. The fun part of filmmaking is the conceiving and the shooting, but you have to do the press because you want people to see your film.

The Uses of Rehearsal

I would love to shoot a film in the order that it is written, but I've never had that luxury. It is very hard to hold the overall arc of a story together if you shoot out of order over a long period of time. That is why I rehearse. Making *Frida*, I rehearsed with Salma Hayek and Fred Molina for two weeks. We rehearsed in order because we were going to shoot totally out of order. And as a result of that rehearsal, they were able to make their relationship have some depth to it. For example, we shot the most emotional scene in *Frida* — the scene when Frida and Diego split up on the street — the second day of shooting. Because in rehearsal we'd worked on the through-line up to that point, they could feel comfortable playing that emotional high right at the top of the shoot. But when the distributor-producers saw the scene on dailies they thought it was overacted. I kept saying, "No, it's not overacting. What you are looking at is the highest emotional point of the entire film." Later, when it was put in order, it finally made sense. But I still feel that scene could have been better if we had shot it a little bit closer to sequence.

We had a similar problem in *Titus*. Anthony Hopkins kept underplaying the lines that come after his hand is cut off. The first time he did it, he was repressing his rage because he was afraid of the larger-than-life Shakespearean acting style. But his inhibitions prevented him from fulfilling the needs of the scene; he didn't reach what the scene had to be in the context of the whole play. So we talked about it that night and we agreed to reshoot it. But then he went to the other extreme. So in the end that speech was put together in the editing room from five or six takes. I'm not even sure that he could ever do it live because it had such incredible range. We were just blown away by the final result.

Of course, there are also many film actors who have never done theatre and who are terrified of rehearsal. I had that in *Titus*. I had actors who not only had never done Shakespeare, they had never done theatre. Rehearsal was what allowed them to feel the language and make it their own.

There are limits to what you can achieve in rehearsal, of course. With *Titus*, I had all fifteen actors together for three weeks, and it helped us to find the highs and lows. At a certain point, though, Hopkins said, "I can't do this anymore. The coffee cups in the room are bothering me. I need to feel the mud on my face if I am on that crossroads. I need to be in those spaces." So we stopped a half a week early and began to shoot.

Of course, when you rehearse a film, the blocking is very abstract — you're just trying to begin to feel the physicality of the characters. No one is worried about repeating it; it's just to get a sense, just to open up the door so you can see the possibilities. I think that kind of rehearsal allows for much more exploration, much more risk-taking. In rehearsal, it's intimate. It's like theatre. The actors are allowed to make mistakes. I am allowed to question. We can completely go at it.

When film directors don't rehearse, it's either because they don't have money — which is not their fault because producers don't believe it is necessary — or because they are frightened of it. Young directors, or directors who are inexperienced working with actors, worry that if you rehearse, the result won't be spontaneous. That's nonsense. If you rehearse a movie for two or three weeks — and most people don't even get that much — you are doing each scene only once or twice. And by the time you get to shooting any particular scene, it may be months later, in a completely different environment, under unbelievable pressure, where now you've got two hundred people watching. If you don't rehearse and the actors have never had any time to try it out, you get on that set to block for the camera with the pressure of being watched by hundreds while the clock ticks away and the costs mount.

Experienced film directors, especially if they've done some theatre, are comfortable with actors and believe that actors have something to contribute more than just their presence. If you're a director like that, then you want to know if the actors can go somewhere they have never been before; you want to discover. You don't *know* necessarily; you just say, "Let's see if it works." Whereas my impression is that many young film directors — especially those without theatre experience — don't really like working with the actors. That doesn't mean they can't make great films; of course they can. But their work is often less about investigating character, about how to tell the story through human interaction, and more about visual exploration. And so, instead of actively directing the actors, they just cast an actor who has already done the same type of role — someone who they know can repeat what they've already seen. When you cast experienced actors like Meryl Streep or Robert DeNiro, that may work. The director may not get exactly what he or she imagined — and many haven't imagined it at all — but it can work. But you may not be pushing those actors to a new place.

Rehearsal in theatre has a different purpose. The first two or three weeks of rehearsal are just exploring, talking, and discovering. It's open range for potential chaos and possibility. But after those first two or three weeks, as things start to settle, then you need to lock it. So part of rehearsal in theatre is the repetition needed to make it feel solid, because you don't want it to change every single night — not as a director you don't. Yes, you want it to feel alive and you want the actors to feel like they are making it fresh. But, honestly, once you get a good reading, I don't believe any director wants to have it change. It's very frustrating when the actors get it and then lose it.

The Power of Setting

There are stories that are better told in film because the real landscape can be so expressive. One of the things I loved about *Frida* was Mexico. I wanted to show real Mexico in the '20s, the '30s, the actual Teotihuacan. I wanted to be on those pyramids and show the real colors of the real places. I think that is the equivalent in film of that visceral aspect of theatre.

I had the same pleasure with *Titus*. I did *Titus* as a play first, of course, and it's hard to say if I could have made the film otherwise because I learned so much doing it on stage with minimal scenery and just fifteen actors. But once I was making the film, engaged in trying to find the literal but still poetical equivalent of Shakespeare's settings — choosing the backgrounds, filling in those blanks for the audience but still trying to keep mystery and layers of potential meaning — all of that was pure pleasure. I discovered the power of filming the actual Colosseum, Mussolini's palace, or a burnt-out swamp.

Shakespeare's Language on Film

A staging of *Titus* heightens the language in a way that film can't. You simply can't put all that language on film. For instance, I had originally cut one of Marcus's big speeches in half. When we got to shooting it, I had to cut it again. Time is very different in film. Audiences have become so accustomed to fast editing that they get bored if they have to sit and watch one image for a long time while someone is delivering a long speech.

On the other hand, Shakespeare's language comes through better on film. It's difficult for a contemporary audience to get all of Shakespeare unless they have studied it, but as soon as you can see the actors' lips, as you do on film, you can understand what they are saying a hell of a lot better than you do from forty feet away. I think that the film of *Titus* is very clear that way. Even if you don't know what a "weeping welkin" is, you can understand every single thing that is being said on screen because the actors do and because the context can help.

Also on film, Shakespeare's language can be played so much more naturally and under the breath. The language may be heightened, but if you speak it without adding umms and humms, you can stay within the meter and still sound very natural. You learn so much from hearing a genius like Anthony Hopkins delivering that text without having to project to be heard.

Theatre Is the Actor's Medium

Theatre is the actor's medium. Young directors may not be as attracted to theatre as they are to movies, but most actors will do theatre as well as film — so long as they can make a living — because, in film, an actor doesn't really have much control over his performance. That's why Hopkins doesn't do a lot of takes. He doesn't want to give the director a lot of choices; he wants to be the one to decide, "This is it." So he is very prepared, he's rehearsed, he'll nail it on the first take. And if the camera wasn't ready, then he can get fussy and say,

"Well, tough shit. I don't care if it went out of focus. That's my performance and you deal with it."

Race

If you look at the reality of Rome at the time *Titus* is set, there would have been black people present in most of the scenes. But because race was an issue in the play, I chose to have Harry Lennix (who played Aaron both on stage and in the film) be the sole black character. I wanted to make him isolated; I wanted him to be very singular.

But usually, doing Shakespeare, I wouldn't hesitate to cast a black actor in any role. Kenneth Branagh cast Denzel Washington in *Much Ado About Nothing*. Of course, you may have more freedom for that in Shakespeare. You could do it in *Carousel*, but it will have resonance; the audience will think about the sociological ramifications.

The Lion King transcends race; you don't think about who's black and who's white. Or at least white audiences don't. For nonwhite people all over the world — I hear this from African Americans to Maoris — *The Lion King* is very powerful politically. There's a black king on stage. It's a musical that is not about racism, yet the majority of the people are nonwhite. Usually, if you look at a black musical, it's going to be about race. *Ragtime*, Duke Ellington [theatre music], even *Hairspray*, are all about race. *The Lion King* is not about race and, at the same time, it celebrates race. I made a conscious decision — and Disney agreed — that these roles would be played by nonwhite people; they could be Japanese, Hawaiian, Brazilian, but they would not be Caucasian. Though you could call it reverse racism, it just feels right.

We've just opened a production in Australia that I love; there are thirty nationalities in the cast. And the simple fact of having Maoris, Southeast Asians, Brazilians, and Trinidadians together on one stage is very eloquent, I think. I've spent a lot of time in Asia, and I very much appreciate and am inspired by theatre that comes from outside Western culture. I am gratified that *The Lion King* has that wide appeal — that it is not just a display of an American piece of theatre, but is owned by wherever it is. It is German in Germany; it is Australian in Australia.

Theatre that Television Could Do Better

When I was in Indonesia — and I don't know what it is like anymore — they didn't have TV and film, so theatre was part of day-to-day life. Theatre met different needs: there was sacred theatre and then there was theatre that was just pure fun. Here, the equivalent of that is television. And television here is ubiquitous in the same way; it's just part of living. I don't watch these things, but if you watch *Friends* or *The Sopranos*, the characters become as familiar to you as the characters in the *Ramayana* and *Mahabharata* were in Indonesia.

But theatre is varied here, too, even despite television. You've still got silly comedies and you've got trite musicals and some that have a little bit of content here and there, and then you've got heavy plays like *Homebody/Kabul*. Off-Broadway and Off-Off-Broadway, there's experimental theatre still, though maybe not on the scale of the '60s and '70s, which is when I grew up in the theatre. My favorite theatre is the work of artists like Robert Lepage or Theatre Complicité, or Peter Brook's experiments from time to time — artists who are able to mix the worlds of reality and surreality. That's what interests me in the theatre. I don't like to see theatre that television could do better. I don't especially want to watch people sitting on couches in living rooms or pretending to cook with a stove that works. You go to a play that might have a very realistic, elaborate set of a front porch and right away you think — or, as a theatre artist, *I* think — "Oh hell," because you know you're going to be sitting on that front porch for the next two to three hours, stuck in a certain kind of reality. And, yes, the actors can be wonderful, the direction of the actors can be wonderful, but I know what kind of world I'm going into from the onset. When I walk in to a theater to see a live production I want to be transported to a world that is thoroughly surprising and illuminating.

9
Maggie Gyllenhaal

Maggie Gyllenhaal is an American actor whose film work includes the lead role in Steven Shainberg's Secretary, *with James Spader, as well as supporting roles in Mike Newell's* Mona Lisa Smile, *starring Julia Roberts, and Spike Jonze's* Adaptation. *In 2004, she gave an acclaimed performance as Priscilla, The Homebody's daughter, in a production of Tony Kushner's play* Homebody/Kabul, *which also starred Linda Emond. It played first at the Mark Taper Forum in Los Angeles and then at the Brooklyn Academy of Music (BAM) in New York. When this interview was conducted in Los Angeles in August of 2004, she had just finished shooting Laurie Collyer's* Shall Not Want.

Control

You can give a performance on film that's really shifted when it's finally put together, based on someone else's idea of what you should or shouldn't be doing or what the movie is about. That can be an amazing feeling, or it can be really horrible. I'm learning to let go of what I've done after I've finished it because it's really out of my control. I'm starting to think, almost as a way of protecting myself, that the process of making movies has to be more important than the product.

That's true in the theatre, too, but in a very different way. One of the things that was so great about *Homebody/Kabul* was that Tony [Kushner] really put it in our hands. That was especially true of the ending of the play. If we didn't enter into that last scene totally open and clear about where we were coming from — which might shift every single night depending on what happened in the rest of the performance — and really listening and focusing on each other, then we didn't get to a place where the play had an ending. You could find the meaning of the scene only by letting go of everything; the play required that you relinquish control to something artistic. And by writing an ending that required the actors to be really at the top of their form, Tony forced it to be about the process as opposed to the product. And there would be nights when the play would have no ending, but he trusted us to work that way; he put into our hands the fate of his play.

Getting Your Own Coffee

On a movie set, actors are treated with an incredible amount of respect and, at the same time, sometimes infantilized. It's like, "Let me do everything for you. Let me get you a cup of coffee," and, mixed with that, "Oh, here, don't walk across the street by yourself because you might walk into a car." That happens not because all movie actors are spoiled, but because moves are made very fast and the set has to function almost like a well-oiled machine. No human stuff can be allowed to get in the way of that. And if you're an actor, it's a strange conflict because you're working in an environment that has to function almost like the army, and yet you're asked in your work to be totally human and available at any minute.

Now, I understand why it works that way on a tiny movie, where I've got to change my clothes in the closet and then wipe off this lipstick and put on different color lipstick while looking at the script real quick because we're filming the next scene in ten minutes. You really have no time and you are constantly working, for twelve hours straight, so it's someone's job to do little things for you to help you function. And I understand that, as long as you're respectful and don't think you deserve that because you are somehow better than anyone else. But on a big movie, where you have three days to shoot one scene, I don't really understand why you can't just get your own coffee.

With a play, the rehearsal schedule is just much more human. You get there at eleven and you're done at six. And there's no reason why anyone should bring you anything because you are going to work for two hours and then you are going to have a union-regulated break and you can go get your coffee. It's set up so everyone can do their own dirty work.

Getting What You Need

To the limited extent I've seen diva behavior on a set, it did not come from Julia Roberts. She has enough power that she doesn't need to throw a tantrum to get the things that she needs. The people who were confident with the work they were doing and confident that they had the power they needed to give a performance they had control over — those people behaved respectfully. The diva behavior came from actors who were uncomfortable with their position and insecure about how much power they had.

I do think that actresses have, in the past, had very little power in film — even women who were very famous and very rich — so that the only way that they could maintain some control was by demanding it. I don't think that is necessary now in the way that it maybe was in the '60s and before, or even the '80s. I'm sure that it was very difficult for women to have any degree of control over their performance; and if, as a result, they screamed and yelled a little bit about how mistreated and not listened to they felt, they were called divas. I think maybe that behavior was misconstrued by the people who were keeping them from the things they needed artistically.

You know, before Linda Emond did The Homebody's monologue in *Homebody/Kabul*, she wasn't outside laughing and joking with everybody; she was working and preparing because she knew that, at a particular time, she was going to go on stage for a specific amount of time. Whereas, working on a huge movie — where maybe you'll shoot a very small amount each day and maybe they will tell you, "You have fifteen minutes until you have to work," but really, they won't call you for an hour and a half while they get the lights set up — it's hard to remain in that focused place for the entire time. And a lot of people on movies — just like in theatre, just like anywhere — don't really understand what it means to remain focused and ready to work at any moment, so they'll come in and say, "Oh hey, what's up?" and you'll have to find a kind and clear way of saying, "Actually, it may not look like I'm working, but I am."

But I think that's easier to do now. I think my generation is coming at it from a different place. And you do have to assert that power sometimes. As a young actress, I feel that I have to make it clear early on that it is not going to work for me if someone says, "Go stand over there and smile." That's not how I act or how I work; if that's how a director works, I can't do that. You have to be really clear about working with people who want to collaborate with you.

Of course, in theatre there's no reason to fight for control of your performance. There is no reason to manipulate anybody. There's no reason to yell at anybody. In the end, it's your performance and you are going to be the one standing on the stage giving it, so there's no reason to have a fight with anybody about it.

Fame

I think the effect of fame depends on what you become famous for. Holly Hunter or Meryl Streep or Debra Winger are actresses who became famous for being good actresses, not for having a specific "quality." They became famous for frequently taking risks. That, I think, only helps you.

Work and Lifestyle

I find life in the theatre to be much healthier than in film. In the theatre, you can completely dive into a character and still live your life well. With film, I find that very hard. In the theatre, you simply have to take care of yourself. In *Homebody/Kabul*, I definitely felt Priscilla all over me, all inside me, in both a very light and exhilarated way and also in a very dark place. But in order to do the play, I had to take care of myself; otherwise, I simply couldn't do it. I've felt this about everything I've done on stage, that I really had to be in strong, good physical condition.

And I think it's actually the same way in film, but I find it much harder to maintain. In the theatre, you can make yourself a sandwich from your own refrigerator and bring it to work with you. On a movie set — especially the set of a little movie, which is mostly what I've chosen to do — the food is disgusting, but you have to eat for sustenance. You could bring a sandwich from home, but that means you'd have to wake up at 4:00 in the morning, and, sorry, I'm going to sleep as long as I can. You get picked up at 5:15 in the morning, so you wake up at 4:45, take your shower, and get ready, and you work until 6:30 at night, and you get home at 7:00, you eat something, and you pass out. It takes a huge effort for that lifestyle not to disrupt your life. You're in a kind of crisis mode, which can really feed you, but which isn't that healthy. And because of that, you're more likely to lose yourself. I'm still titillated by the idea of getting sucked into another character, but I don't think it's actually the wisest way of working.

Love Scenes

If you do a movie and you have to do a love scene with somebody, you do it once and maybe do it, like, for three hours and it's over. Doing it in a play, you do it every single day, which is kind of strange. It is maybe harder to keep those boundaries clear when you are working on stage; you have to figure out a way to be clear about that. That's something maybe a little less healthy in theatre than in film.

Technique and Instinct

When I was doing *Homebody/Kabul* in New York, I kept imagining the audience saying, "Oh, you're a film actress. Let's see if you can pull this off." I had actually done theatre all the way through college. I didn't go to a conservatory, but I studied here and there. I'm young, so in that sense I'm inexperienced, but, if I had any training at all, it was in the theatre. So, actually, it was doing film that was very strange and different. But whether it had to do with my film career or not, I was a young, new actress taking on this huge thing — a major role in a major Tony Kushner play — and if I were in the audience, I would say, "Let's see if this person can do this." I think that's fair, and I was asking myself that, too, the whole time I was doing it: "Can I do this? Can I do this well?"

And I look at Linda Emond, who has this incredible amount of experience and training and discipline. I would watch the kind of warm-ups that she does. I just don't do that, you know. I was very curious about it and I would watch her, and I've picked some of it up on my way here and there, but I work in a different way. When I first got onto the BAM stage, the most natural and organic part of me went, "This is incredible. This space feels great. I love it here." But there's another part of me that went, "Oh, look at Linda sitting on stage in her chair bouncing her voice off the walls. I don't know how to do that at all." There's something terrifying to me about that. So sometimes I think I should empower myself by learning more about how to use my voice, my breath; why not have every tool I can possibly have? I see how helpful it is.

That kind of work will also help me with the thing I was talking about, about getting lost in a character. It is important to be able to remain objective about the work and, at the same time, give yourself over to it completely. I haven't been able to master that. I can give myself over, but then I tend to lose my balance.

But I'm working and I'm learning. That's part of what I mean when I say I am much more interested in the process than in the actual product. I will look at a performance of mine in a film and say, "Wow, look at what I've learned since I made this." It's the only way I can avoid being really judgmental of my work — to think about the way I worked, what I was gripping on to, what I was loose about, and then say, "I'm learning."

When I did *Secretary*, I thought I really understood intellectually what was happening at every moment. But ultimately what's good about that performance is where I *think* I've got it all under control, but actually I'm overwhelmed. It's that kind of instinctual stuff — stuff that's bigger than my brain — that is actually the best work.

Lately, I don't really think there is any such thing as bad acting. I think acting is whatever you are feeling. If you are clear about the text, if you know what the circumstances are and what you need as a character, then whatever you feel — if you feel self-conscious and don't know where to put your feet, if you feel so angry at the person you are in the scene with and that wasn't what you had expected, even if you are doing everything you can not to feel the way you feel because you don't think you are supposed to — any of that is fine.

Rehearsing

In a play, you rehearse so much that you can throw it away again. With movies, I prefer not to rehearse — or, at least, I prefer to rehearse in my own way, which is much more introspective and unconscious. With film, what often happens is that you have a week to rehearse or a few days and you can just get stuck in something that's very static without having enough time to come around the other side again. It is better for me to just throw myself into it.

In the movie I just finished, *Shall Not Want*, there's a scene at the end that I was always really worried about. It's a beautiful script, but there's one scene that I felt was kind of incomplete. So we'd shot most of the movie already — we were maybe halfway through the last week of a five-week shoot. It was the night before we were going to shoot this scene, and I sat down with it at like eight o'clock, having just come home from a day of shooting, and thought, "I'm going to work this through. I'm going to figure it out." And then I realized that, actually, that's not how it works on a movie. I cannot figure this scene out until I'm there outside with the six-year-old actress who is playing my daughter, who may or may not be upset and crying. I need to know if it's hot. Or is it cold? What does the car look like that we're trying to get in and out of? I realized that intellectualizing my way through it, or even analyzing it as a text, really wasn't the way to work it. I actually felt proud of myself for saying, "I'm going to put it down. We're going to have to hack our way through it on the set tomorrow, and it's going to take a little more time than everyone's going to want it to, but that's the only way this is going to work."

I don't think that's true in the theatre. I can't imagine going on stage without really having worked something through. At least a piece of that has to do with having to create your own environment in the theatre. You are working in an imaginary space, and you have to create the world that you are in. Whereas, when you make a film, you know that eventually it's going to be pouring rain, nighttime, and you are going to be in a castle on a hill somewhere, so you can say, "Okay, let's just wait until we get there and let it play out." If you are on stage and imagining that, then you have to do a different kind of work to make it real.

And it's also because, in theatre, the text requires more work. For instance, with a text like Tony's, the twists and turns of it require you to make some decisions together about what each scene is about. The meaning of each scene shifted very much after we had analyzed the text together, which didn't really, truly happen until we got to New York. Whereas often in film, it's not about the language; it's about some kind of real human interaction. And of course theatre is about that, too, but in theatre you are using language to create an environment, so you have to look at it as a text.

Audiences

The New York and L.A. audiences for *Homebody/Kabul* were really different. I was so disappointed by the audiences in Los Angeles, I can't even tell you. It wasn't entirely their fault because I don't think our production of the play was completely working when we were there. But we were playing to half-full houses and I would feel them trail off and get confused and lost. I'm sure there were many people in there who followed it all the way through, but I felt that the audience as a whole was really scattered. I would just lose them, they would just fly away, is how it felt. A friend of mine came to see the play in L.A. and told me that she overheard someone in the bathroom saying, "This isn't a play. This a political treatise," or something like that — as if the two things couldn't fit in the same place.

So when we first started in New York, I couldn't believe it; this audience followed everything, and they would gasp and they would giggle and they would moan. It felt like they wanted to let me know that they were with me. And since my character was the one you are following through the play, almost like a narrator, it meant a lot if they were with me. They would laugh at something in a scene or gasp and it would fill my tank, you know. I would think, "Okay, well, I've got all that energy with me and we're going to continue on until the next hard place." And there were places where I would feel them get tired and I would feel them go, "Oh God, what is happening? Pull us through," and I would say to myself, "We're getting through this hard part. You're going to have some relief. It's coming up, it's coming up. I'm going to get it to you. We're going to get it together." And we would carry each other all the way through till the end. And that was just a completely different thing than the L.A. experience.

The audience is a huge part of every performance for me. Just the energy of it. If what you are trying to do all the time is acknowledge everything that is going on around you, then that must include the house, the fact that there are a thousand people out there. They became all sorts of things for me. Sometimes they were Kabul, sometimes they were my mother, sometimes they were my enemy. I felt much more antagonistic toward the audience in L.A. They were a different kind of mother; they were a different kind of Afghanistan. It shifted the play for me a little bit, and I just let it shift. But it does make it harder to want to do another play in L.A.

I was born in New York, but I grew up in L.A., and so I know L.A. pretty well. And I know that there are a lot of really smart and interesting people who live here. But I guess I feel like there's something missing here. I can't live here, you know. And I was really, really disappointed by how hard it was to get these audiences to invest in something that was hard. Because, of course, that's when you are rewarded, that's when you can have a really exciting theatrical experience — when you invest in something that is hard.

I remember when we were maybe a week or two into the *Homebody* rehearsals in New York, and I went to see Simon Russell Beale in Tom Stoppard's *Jumpers*. Someone took me with them on the spur of the moment, and we ran to the theatre and I sat down and I started watching the play with just a piece of me. It was a Sunday night, and I had had a full week of really intense rehearsals that were exercising every part of me, including my brain, and I was just so tired. And then all of a sudden, I went, "Okay, okay, I need to actually engage in order to watch this play, you know. Otherwise, why am I here? What the fuck am I doing?" It was the same with Craig Lucas's play, *Small Tragedies*. I walked in after a day of using half my brain and realized about ten minutes in that I would need to bring more than that to this play. That's an experience I love.

But it's an experience I guess a lot of people in Los Angeles weren't used to and were not interested in having. I know the production of *Homebody/Kabul* in L.A. wasn't perfect, but it was interesting, I think, and really ambitious, so what the fuck? Wake up and pay attention.

10
David Leveaux

David Leveaux is an associate director at the Donmar Warehouse in London and the founder of Theatre Project Tokyo. He has directed extensively in London, including for the Almeida Theatre, the Royal Shakespeare Company, and the National Theatre. His work on Broadway includes Tony-nominated productions of Anna Christie *(1993), starring Natasha Richardson and Liam Neeson;* The Real Thing *(2000), starring Stephen Dillane;* Nine *(2003), starring Antonio Banderas; and* Jumpers *(2004), starring Simon Russell Beale. At the time of this interview in the spring of 2001, he was working on a rewrite of a screenplay for a planned production of* Therese Raquin *that had been in the works for a number of years.*

Emulation

There was a three-day conference called "Future Directions" put together largely by the Society of West End Theatres. I was on a panel titled, "What Can the Theatre Learn from the Current Popularity of Cinema?" The presumption of the conference was that the theatre hasn't got its act together in the same way that film has. It's difficult not to go into a situation like that without finding yourself defending the theatre. I think a lot of people wanted to say, "We're not the poor cousins of the film industry, and we have a different set of obligations." And the film people inevitably were saying, "Yes, but look at the diminishing audience you play to, both in terms of class group and age." But what theatre can't do is emulate film directly on any front. That's what was problematic about the conference. There are some things we can learn. Some film people are terrific on the practical front. But they make their effects through different means.

The one thing we share is that when a movie comes out that's a big hit, it's a huge event; everyone wants to see it. The theatre needs to be an event as well. In a sense it needs to be more of an event because it can happen only once a night and it can happen only in that particular place. People have to go to that place and see it.

I think there's a danger that we take the idea of theatre for granted, as if there's something holy about its existence which leads us to become complacent: "It's clearly a good thing. Pity that no one is coming." It's only a good thing if it's capable of showing us who we are.

Conviction

Theatre people are staggeringly realistic, almost ruthlessly so. The entire time that I've worked in the theatre, there's been a genuine passion for the work itself and a belief in that work which comes from the very center of the process. Otherwise it simply doesn't happen. Theatre is made only on the cusp of conviction; it's only made there. Whereas in my long but insubstantial relationship with the film industry — which has gone on for eight years as I've been trying to make this film, *Therese Raquin* — although I've met all kinds of very interesting, very enlightened people along the way, I have to say that in the industry overall there is the most enormous kind of guessing game going on.

The Stakes

In the making of a film, you're talking about millions of dollars at stake. The stakes are very high financially. But they're not actually as high as some people think they are. They're not actually *that* high. The reality is that, yes, if you make enough films, you're going to have a lot of failures, but you're also going to have some successes. And if you have a small number of successes, success on that level, financially speaking, is just massive. You should measure the amounts people have to put up to make a movie against the amounts they can probably expect to make over time. How many movies do what *Heaven's Gate* did? Whereas the margins are much tinier within the theatre and therefore just as critical, if not more so. The fact is that the wrong show at the wrong time can bring a theatre to its knees. A bad movie is not going to bring Universal Studios to their knees. It just isn't. And I guarantee that, for an actor, to be in a not-so-great movie that lives and dies with almost the same speed as the life cycle of a dragonfly is preferable to the experience of dying in a big way on a Broadway stage. So I think there's a bit of a cliché about that. It's just to do with the absolute amounts of money involved.

Interlopers

In film, there are many people involved in the process who don't have anything to do with actually creating this thing at all, but who have an unreasonable influence on how it's created. I'm talking about lawyers, producers, and especially agents — powerful agents who are infinitely more present in the process of filmmaking than they ever would be in the theatre. And they can be very unhelpful. They can withhold their client from a project which they perceive to be not in the interests of the business which is their agency. It can be done in many subtle ways; they can simply refuse to cooperate. I didn't realize just how much people worry about agents in the film business, much more than we tend to in the theatre. In an earlier incarnation of *Therese Raquin*, we had some producers (no longer on the project) who were accustomed to working with agents in a certain way that I found utterly untenable. They gave agents enormous power in the situation. There was a deference to the agent: "Why don't you speak to so and so? Why didn't you speak to that agent?" I don't speak to agents. I just don't. Why? Because it's got absolutely nothing whatever to do with the thing one's doing. Nothing. The only reason you're going to talk to an agent is to prevent this person from fucking it up. And I think it's interesting that people deal across desks much more in the film business, whereas in the theatre everybody's much closer to the rehearsal room.

Trying to Make a Film

So why make a film? I love the medium and always have done. But for a long time, I didn't think about working in it. And I certainly wasn't going to make a film just for the sake of making a film, because I was, and always have been, gripped by making theatre. If I just keep doing that for the rest of my life, it will never cease to fascinate and puzzle and frustrate and energize me. So it's not a reaction against that.

What happened in this case was that there was this story, *Therese Raquin*, which I had done in the theatre and which struck me as being something that could be done fantastically in film because it's an interior story, really. It's the story about someone whose project is love, whose talent is loving, and about just how radical and difficult and sometimes morally challenging such a person can be. And I thought, "Well, I'd like to see that in images that are THIS BIG," because it needed a close-up to see that. It needed a close-up of that face, again and again and again, while our perception of who she is keeps changing.

But the process of setting up the film, for all sorts of reasons, took so long, the ups and downs of it all, that I've just recently found myself wondering whether in fact it is something that I want to make, or in what form. But in that process, during the search to make this film, things have attached. And one of those things is a development deal with USA Films. So suddenly I'm thinking about films beyond *Therese Raquin*. But it wasn't that I set out to get into film. I just wanted to make *Therese Raquin* as a film. Lots of people do these things differently. You know, Sam Mendes would make a very clear decision that where he was headed was film. Not that he didn't love the theatre. He does. But film was where he was going. And he seemed to have a sort of eerie sense of which film it was going to be, and there he was: *American Beauty*. But that's not me at all. I just think you kind of arrive at corners that you go around. I've never actually satisfactorily set out to do something in abstract. It's always been a catastrophe.

This has been a very, very difficult process, though. There have been several bombs dropped into the middle of the proceeding. Kate Winslet has been attached to this. A year ago she got pregnant. So that was it. After seven years of working on this film, it was delayed a year. And the financiers and the producer said, "Oh, that's all right. We'll wait for Kate." And I was happy in one sense about that because I want to work with Kate. But there was another part of me that was feeling that there's something wrong. There's a feeling of vitality that drove this thing forward for a certain period that I don't have [in] quite the same way. And yet, ironically, the film is chugging along. It's got its money; it can definitely be made. There is an oddity about this.

And there have been various phases, including being called at four in the morning every single morning when I was in Tokyo by Los Angeles lawyers literally threatening me because there was something I wouldn't give in on in terms of the structure of the movie. And they've actually said this to me [*in an exaggerated American accent*], "David, you have to understand how this town works." And I finally realized that — and I said it on this occasion — "The mistake you're making is to assume that I'm desperate to make this movie regardless. And I suspect that's the world you live in — so that from that first power lunch, a director of a film will do anything to keep it going. The thing is …" (and I did say this to this lawyer) "that is your only power, and you don't have it. Because, while I want to make this movie very, very much, I don't want to make it at any cost. It has to be that movie, or it's not a movie I want to make. That's it." When I finally said that, silence for two weeks. And then the matter was dropped. So you have to be very careful about being swept up. Everybody thinks there's a train moving out of the station.

And that is a big difference between film and theatre. Because when those amounts of money are involved, either something falls through and nobody quite knows why, or things have a way of gathering a head of steam even though nobody really knows anymore why they're making this particular film. And that's a very dangerous place to be.

Incompleteness and Meaning

Theatre functions by image first and foremost. It's simply not true to say that it's primarily a linguistic, primarily a text medium. It just isn't. It is perhaps in the main more wordy than film, but even that depends on what you mean. There's what I would call a "landscape" in any great play, which means that the experience of the play is not entirely attributable simply to the surface structure of the language.

There's a much larger subject here, which is how we perceive language in the theatre. It is possible to create a moment on the stage which is a coalescence of rhythm, sense, tempo, and silence. Theatre always tends towards silence, I think. And if so, why is it so different from this thing we call the non-linguistic medium: image?

In cinema, you bring one image against another, and — at least in a great film — something in the process by which you connect those two images is where the event, the experience of the film, lies. And that's exactly the way it's done in theatre. As soon as you try to make something literal in the theatre, it dies. If you attempt to make it conclusive, coherently represented, complete, it dies. Because as soon as you complete the circuit on stage, the audience becomes redundant. They feel it, though they may not know why; there's nothing they bring to that moment. The theatre depends on being incomplete. It depends on suggestion.

But so does the cinema. If it's a good movie, it triggers my imagination, I do participate. I know that the thing is a closed world, but I am participating; I am making connections between things that are not necessarily told. Think about the films of Eric Rohmer — talk about incomplete! Those chamber stories he tells; even when people go out on the road or go into a public park, you never really see anyone else. It's always kind of like on Mars. I remember a wonderful shot: this girl — her boyfriend had just left her — is in this clean, exquisite, steely white apartment and she's just sitting there obviously thinking about her boyfriend, and hanging on the wall is a red towel. And it's so beautifully done. It's shot in natural light with an open lens; it's the eye, and yet of course it's highly poetic.

Just the other day I was looking at a detail in Mike Leigh's *Topsy Turvy*. Mike Leigh is a scrupulous director; you see why he adores film. There is an incredible shot in *Topsy Turvy* — it's something he points out on a DVD that's got his own commentary. He's kind of chattering along as the movie goes on. It's fascinating. He's talking about how at the beginning there's a lot of exposition you have to get through, a lot of information you have to get out somehow, and at the same time keep it funny, keep it interesting. And then you get to the point where, okay, the exposition is done, we've got the information, and now we're going to the heart of what this is about. And there's this really wonderful shot of Sullivan, clearly in an unsatisfactory marriage where something isn't shared. His wife is lying on this four poster bed, and he's sitting on the chair talking about the libretto, and he stands up and the shot is, as it were, over her shoulder, and you can see that along the edge of the canopy of the bed there's this lace trim. And so the trim sort of fringes his head. And the sense of the barrier between these two quite different worlds, and his inability to enter this one, is just immense. That's an instance where it's not that a detail is missing, but where the particular detail you're looking at, and why, has great power. So I don't know that the very fact that the entire picture has to be filled in film, that there can be no blank spaces, necessarily means that you're stuck with what I would call literalism. There's literal theatre and there's literal filmmaking.

Psychology vs. Rhythm

There's that scene in *Good Will Hunting* where the psychiatrist is talking about the death of his wife, all that she meant to him. You can get away with it in the movies, but try that in theatre! It would die. It would be risible. You wouldn't get away with it in the theatre because the theatre's a more brutal place. It won't stand up to sloppy introspection. It will stand up to introspection, but the introspection's got to be tough, urgent, and interrogative: "To be or not to be. That is the question." But the kind of neo-Freudian obsession with feeling, with self, the absolute primacy of the individual's feeling, the "sacredness" of individualism — all that is absolutely the death of the theatre. You won't get theatre that way.

Years ago, I did a production of Eugene O'Neill's play, *Moon for the Misbegotten*. We had three wonderful actors, and I remember saying to them one day, "Look, I'm going to ban the word psychology from this rehearsal room. This play has nothing to do with psychology; not a single word of this play would stand up in court, psychologically. If you look for the meaning there, you'll find that it's inane, heavy, clumsy, and overlong. Instead, you must see it as a piece of music. The first act is an allegro, in a major key, with a couple of notes here and here, probably from the cellos, that seem to be in a minor key (that seems to be out of synch, don't know what it is, find out later). Act II, allegretto. That minor key comes back a couple of more times but in a slightly more developed form. (What is that?) Act III, great love scene, adagio. Suddenly that theme that was so compressed opens out. And Act IV, coda. So we're going to do this completely as if it were a piece of music." And the actors really went there with it. And in those circumstances, but only in those circumstances, O'Neill's plays lift. It's amazing. Not a word stands up in court, but there's no doubt that there's authentic poetry.

The same with Stoppard's *The Real Thing*. There were scenes that were more free form than other scenes, but overall it was almost like jazz. We went through the process of saying, "This scene is in 3/4. This is in 2/4. This has to happen there. That absolutely requires you to be there, so maybe there's another way you could do that." Usually I'm very keen, even if it takes a long time in rehearsal, to find where a person needs to be at a certain point. But in this case, some aspects of it never stopped changing. It was a big journey; it never stopped. From the Donmar to the Albery to New York. And it took us a while to get New York because things had to go at a slightly different tempo. Things that could be dealt with very quickly for an audience here in London needed to be marked. Other things that we marked more here were picked up so quickly in New York that we could move on. It went on and on throughout the preview process in New York; we were finding and finding.

It was really quite testing, but worth it because of what we got in return, especially from the lead actor, Stephen Dillane. Stephen is uncanny. He has this recorder in his head, and he can come off stage and know exactly where something worked or didn't work. He's incredibly clever. That extraordinary speech of the cricket bat — the technical skill behind what he was doing was just blinding. By which I mean, the management of rhythm, of sense, the ability to slightly accelerate. On a good night, he would land the end of that speech absolutely as if it'd been a rock and roll song.

And he will never ignore anything. For an actor acting with Stephen, you can find it very difficult or you can actually get high on it. Because Stephen will cancel nothing. Nothing that you do will be rejected or blocked. In the end, what happened was that the whole company was able to play jazz. It was a great moment when everybody realized that they'd reached that point where it was absolutely possible to live on stage and the thing wasn't going to fall away underneath them. But you've got to get through the fear of falling.

It's true that actors won't be happy in rehearsals unless you talk about the psychological syntax of a scene, but ultimately I do it only because I know it's something that the modern actor needs as a tool. I don't believe in it. I don't believe in it as having anything to do with the actual experience of a moment of theatre. I think it's a way for actors to reach a point of some kind of provisional certitude which enables them to become free. But ultimately theatre is not about psychology; it's about rhythm. There is not a single thing that will move you in the theatre unless the rhythm is right. It's brutal like that. Rhythm is the connection to the invisible world in theatre.

The Human Voice and Technology

Theatre is like music — like live music, which is of an altogether different order than recorded music. The actual presence in the room of something vibrating against something else, which creates a sound which reaches your ear, that's the stuff of theatre to me. The theatre depends on the sensation of the nontechnically projected form of the human voice.

But the general level of noise in the world we live in is much greater now than it was even ten or twenty years ago, so that the relative proportion of the human voice against the background of other sound was much greater in the past than it is now. And that's a problem for an art form that depends on the human voice. Probably the single greatest problem that we have is preserving any interest in that in a time when the human voice can be distorted, pumped up, comes out of our TVs, comes out of huge speakers. We want bigger, louder. That's just a fact about how the world goes.

And the more you do it, the harder it is to go back. We did a production of *Nine* here in London, and then we did it a few months later in Buenos Aires. And I was appalled that in every theatre we went into, the amplification of voices was so huge. It was distorting. You could see the microphones; in fact, they wanted to show you. They didn't want to disguise these microphones; it was a badge of pride that actors carried these things on their heads. And I cannot but believe that that's in part a product of a militaristic history. It's what happens to a culture when you've been through a period when nobody gives a damn about the human voice. It's actually quite chilling. I must shout so you hear me.

It's interesting to me — I forget who it was who said this, but it struck me as being an incredibly interesting thing — that one of the characteristics of the Nazis, and the way they expressed themselves, was to build bigger and to sound louder. There was a kind of pseudo-Homeric quality. And that was not obviously unique to them, but I'm very, very interested in where the need to do that comes from. Of course it's connected to a certain kind of arrogance, but there's something else behind that. That "bigger and louder" betrays an absolutely catastrophic failure of the imagination. Not only that, but also a deep loathing for the imagination in all of its forms — a sense that imagination makes chaos where there should be order. And fascism is a failure of the imagination and is attractive to people for exactly that reason — either because they're exhausted or because they're lazy. Its attraction is that you don't actually have to do any more thinking.

I'm not saying that because we're creating big, spectacular musicals we're at risk of tumbling into right-wing fascism, but there's something to be learned from this. The more our fascination with technology grows, the more we become aware of what we think is the essential frailty of humanity in comparison with everything else. But it's only frail in one sense. In another sense it's much more powerful.

For instance, I don't have any doubt at all that the voice heals. And I mean that in a completely physiological as well as psychological sense. I don't have any doubt that there are voices that reach into me and there are voices that offend me. Now, why is that? These are certainties. And the loss of interest in the human voice and the potential loss of language I think is a massively concerning thing for those of us in the theatre.

11
Michael Kahn

American theatre and opera director Michael Kahn is the artistic director of the Shakespeare Theatre in Washington, D.C., and director of the drama division of the Juilliard School in New York, where he has been a member of the faculty since the founding of the school in 1968. This interview was conducted in January of 2002.

Media Effects on Theatre

The great thing about television is how much information we have now. In many ways it's limited information, but we have a huge amount of it. Television has done that. On the other hand, television has reduced writing and acting to something smaller than they need to be. That's the size of the television world — small.

Writers are brought up watching television, not going to the theatre. So the culture of theatre writing is changing. The kind of writing that tends to be very popular now, even in the theatre, is a kind of sitcom writing.

Writing for the theatre is so difficult. You can work on a play for so many years, it can get done once, it can close in three days, not get optioned — so it's really difficult for the writers. But I'm somewhat disturbed by the fact that, although there are plays being written about serious issues, there's this enormous need to "sitcom" them.

As far as acting goes, television is both a helpful and an unhelpful influence. Television has helped a lot of people discover their comedic abilities because there is so much comedy on television that young actors have a pretty quick sense of timing and a kind of comedy. But television is not helpful with significant theatre literature, and therefore the people who want to do that don't have very many role models to look up to. In television you tend to play yourself. The unhelpful part of that is that there's not much investigation of character and certainly very little investigation of size or scope. Television doesn't want to take any chances on an actor trying to become a character. It's so much easier to cast someone who is like the part. Or, worse, to take somebody and write a script supposedly based on their personality; that's the cheapest and easiest way to go. The idea of transforming yourself — which is in the long run what is most fun for an actor and which I think can give them the longest career — is something that television doesn't really encourage.

Mostly in the movies, too, actors tend to play themselves. But I do think that, as a result of our exposure to movie acting, our basic sense of acting is actually realer, more truthful, more connected to the way people behave, so that even not-very-good actors act somewhat naturally. The influence of television is more insidious because there is a style of realism on television that actually has nothing whatsoever to do with the way people behave in real life but which seems natural. I jokingly say we're going to be able to teach realism as a style: we'll do '60s realism and '70s realism and. ... But right now "realism" on television has little to do with the way people behave in their living rooms. And I think television has a greater influence on actors than even movies. Although actors would like to be in movies, what they grow up watching is television.

Slowing Down

Unfortunately, films are mostly getting dumber and dumber. I love to go to the movies, but I'm finding it harder and harder to sit through them. Movies have to appeal to the largest audience possible, obviously, and those audiences are getting younger and younger.

But there's another side to that — a quicker processing, more visually sophisticated audience. And probably a new kind of theatre will come of that — sort of an MTV theatre. There are a lot of people doing that, trying to give you images and text at the same time because the audience can watch it all. How deep that gets, I don't know. Maybe I'm a little old-fashioned there, but I don't like that — certainly I don't like that when it's applied to existing literature. Traditional literature is actually destroyed by that. But new writing and new literature that does that can be very exciting.

Overall, though, I don't think theatre needs to compete with MTV, and I don't think it can do it very well. The brilliance of those media is that they can cut, they can superimpose, but very often they can't really tell stories that involve you.

I'm not against the future, you see, but, in a world that goes this fast, I think maybe the theatre can provide a way to slow down in a very healthy and creative way. Does everything have to be observed so quickly? A show like *Oz*, I liked it when it came out, but now the story's over in two minutes: someone arrives, they're murdered. It's so fast they try to fit twenty stories into an hour. And when it's all over, you've had a lot of sensations, you've absorbed a lot of information, but have you really connected? I'm not sure. And, yes, an audience can absorb more quickly, but how do you make them willing to listen?

Popular entertainment is important. It's not a question of this or that; all of these media are important for the culture and should exist simultaneously. But I think we get more of that than the other — that there's an unmet need. I feel that our audience in Washington is coming to classical plays because they need a more profound or a more personal experience. After September 11, audiences started coming with a greater need for the theatre, and with a need to share an experience in a community. But if we develop an audience that doesn't listen, or listens fast and somewhat superficially, then certain kinds of material will simply no longer be useful.

Character and Text

I don't think the presentation in theatre has to be old-fashioned in order to take time to investigate. There are a lot of ways to do that. I'm finding it tremendously valuable and exciting to work on complex classical texts and explore how to make them meaningful now — which means, to be alive, to be challenging, to be interesting, to be emotionally connected to the audience. How do you do that? That challenge is thrilling for me.

I think the key is being able to deliver the text with all the muscularity and technique of deliberative language, and, at the same time, to inhabit the character. There is a struggle between delivering a text really poetically and also being alive as a character. When it starts to work, it is really thrilling, and when it doesn't, you realize you are on one side or the other of the equation — either delivering the text or delivering the character. Trying to put those two together is actually the thing that interests me most right now as a director. And as a teacher, thinking about how to train actors with enough technique to deliver the language but who can still inhabit the feelings, the emotions, the story line.

Young Actors

The kids coming to our acting program at Juilliard haven't read; they've seen mostly television. There's a lot of information they have at a superficial level, but they certainly haven't read many plays. They are coming to be actors, and some of them, of course, want to be stars. Their heroes are whomever is the major movie star at the moment — Kevin Spacey, Robin Williams. There's no past; there's only the present. So they bring less to the table.

Actors' Agents

Our students get out of school and they get an agent and the agent won't let them do any theatre — actually stops them! The young actress who just played Ophelia for us in Washington was told that if she stayed on to play Juliet, her agent would drop her. That's not chopped liver to play Juliet in a major Shakespeare theatre, but they told her they'd drop her unless she came back to New York to be available for pilot season.

Or agents will not tell their clients when they're offered a job in theatre. It doesn't happen only to young actors. I offered Christopher Walken *Macbeth*. I've known Christopher a long time. I saw him later and said, "Gee, I was really sorry you couldn't do it." He said he never heard about it. He called and screamed at his agent.

I guess agents are under greater pressure than ever before. They're also about twelve years old and haven't got a clue why anybody would want to do Juliet or Macbeth. So, that's a new thing, and it's a pernicious thing.

Openness

Theatre is one place that people don't lose jobs based on their opinions or their feelings. Why are there more homosexuals in the theatre than in movies? You can work in the theatre if you are known to be homosexual; whereas in the movies, people won't hire you. Just try to name six major homosexual film actors. You say, "But we wouldn't know if they're homosexual." That's the point.

Directors Doing Both

For young stage directors, people under thirty or thirty-five, doing film is a huge desire because film is a director's medium. No actor will tell you it's an actor's medium. Every actor will tell you that they enjoy doing it, but they know their performance is at the mercy of the director and the editor. But as a director in film, you can do a lot of things that you simply can't do in the theatre, so I think all young directors probably really want to make movies. I think the best career would be to move back and forth if you can. When I was starting out, certainly theatre directors were theatre directors, film directors were film directors. But now, I think, the healthiest thing is to do a little bit of everything. The British directors get a chance to do everything, don't they? They get to do Shakespeare, they get to do Broadway, they get to do movies. That's probably ideal.

No Longer a Popular Art

The theatre is, perhaps mistakenly, trying to compete with film, so that productions seem to be more and more about spectacle, about effects. The movies can do that so much better that to think audiences need to have that experience replicated in theatres is shortsighted. The theatre is finally going to have to decide what it offers that's different from film and find the audience that wants that.

I think the theatre should define itself differently and accept that maybe it's going to have a smaller audience. Maybe it's not going to be the great popular art it was fifty years ago, before television, when film was less dominant; maybe it's going to be a theatre of tomorrow, which will be smaller theatres reaching fewer people but reaching the people who want something else. That wouldn't be the end of the world. It would just be different.

12
Adrian Lester

British actor Adrian Lester has acted extensively on stage, including the title roles in Henry V, *directed by Nicholas Hytner at the National Theatre, and* Hamlet, *in the touring production directed by Peter Brook; and as Rosalind in the Cheek by Jowl production of* As You Like It. *His film roles include Henry Burton in Mike Nichols'* Primary Colors. *At the time of this interview in the summer of 2004, he was preparing to shoot the second six-part installment of a BBC television series called* Hustle.

Different Theatres

The stage work I've done has mainly been in larger venues; I've only done a few things in smaller houses. Your acting subtly changes depending on the size of the theatre and the type of play. To generalize, I would say that what you do on stage with a cannon, you can do on screen with a laser. But if the audience are close enough to the action and the language of the play is akin to everyday speech then, in the theatre, you can reach your audience with the small, laser-like precision normally reserved for screen work.

The Close-Up on Stage

The actors are not at all in control of the recorded medium. A TV director once said to me, "I can use the editing and camera angles to make you look good or evil, threatening or … well, anyway I want." That is not true of the theatre. On stage, the actors are in control of the volume, the editing (to a certain extent), and the camera angles, so to speak. You create the close-up; you create the long shot. You do it with your place on the stage and the degree of stillness in and around you. The audience can strain forward in order to catch a particular nuance of expression and then, in the same evening, lean back in their seats while a powerful moment of the play unfolds before them.

There is also an invisible cut from one actor to another on stage. What is said or done to you on stage must be received not only by the person you are playing but by the audience also. This requires you to allow the audience and your character to focus on the other actors; there is a delicate shift in status that must be allowed to happen. For you, the scene takes place in the other actor's face and vice versa. If you try (as many do) to retain the focus all the time, you walk all over the invisible cut and you're upstaging. While you're busy looking good, some necessary part of the drama is lost.

Versatility

It always takes me a day or two to adjust to working on the screen when I have just finished a play. In film, every moment of every scene is shot and then repeated from different angles. There is no flow. In a play, any emotions that build over the two hours or so of performance can be explored and then reexplored from night to night in the theatre, making your portrayal stronger and perhaps deeper each time you do it. But on screen there is no such build. Screen actors must create that seeming element of flow during weeks of shooting a story that is invariably shot out of sequence.

Actors who are stage animals can be fantastic on screen, as long as they can let go of the technical elements they normally use in the theatre and deal with the fact that nothing happens in sequence. Also, in film, the audience are down the barrel of the lens. They are very, very close, so that even if the feelings are found at a moment's notice, they have to be honest and real.

The Pleasure and Pain of Permanence

Whatever work you do on stage, no matter how brilliant, soulful, or deeply felt, is gone as soon as the last night is over. It disappears. I always regret that. It's a real shame to have nothing but a memory left of work you are proud of. I would like to have something left, just to say, "I was there. I did that."

On the other hand, the film work you do is always there. It's always accessible. Of course, there are performances you do on film that you wish had been on stage because then they wouldn't stick around to haunt you: "Hey, Adrian. We've got a little clip from … ." "Oh, my God, no. Please say you haven't got *that!*"

Slumming It

Just like any other business, there are some jobs you have to bite the bullet and just *do*. And, truthfully, I haven't done enough of the crap for it to stop being fun. We offer a service. We entertain people. That's our job. Sometimes the audience don't want foie gras; sometimes they just want chips and beer. It's great if the kind of work you do makes the public think and remember. That's good. But sometimes they just want to laugh and forget. And if, while you are slumming it, your face is on billboards everywhere, that's good slumming. The more people know your face a little, the less the people who do the casting are going to be afraid of using you.

Mediocre Text, Mediocre Acting

A lot of actors have tools they use to make something trite and uninteresting sound believable and real. Some may use a certain inflection or a mannerism. Some will behave as though the line spoken to them has struck them in a certain way — it's puzzling or annoying or amusing or whatever. These responses were originally born out of a need for the actor to find a safety net to deal with writing that didn't reach him. But actors can use these tricks again and again until eventually the safety measures become the actor. These actors are easy to spot because their ability to listen truly to their scene partner has become blocked, and every time you see them they react to the other characters around them with the same set of responses. Any real human response is lost in a desire to look good or maintain high status and be interesting on screen.

To get better, you need text that challenges you. You need to play more difficult parts. With good writing, you'll work to get at the bottomless truth of what you are saying. That kind of work opens you up and increases your sensitivity to the art of acting. The text must always leave you working for something. An emotional reaction is what you get when you are busy using the text to change someone.

Pigeonholing

To me, good acting requires that you be aware of what truth you bring to a role so that you can take a hold of that and mold it into a completely different person. You shouldn't be able to do an impression of a particular actor. If you can, it means the same mannerisms come through in every performance. Every role should be completely different; there shouldn't be leftover theatrical residue from one role to another.

You can get pigeonholed quite quickly. The producer, director, casting director, and backers just want to know that the character will be safe in your hands. The best way to assure that is to ask someone who is known for playing those kinds of characters. In *Primary Colors*, I played an Ivy League, preppie, smart, political, young African American. It was my first major role in film. I wasn't known for anything else. Afterward, I realized that only when someone wanted an Ivy League, preppie, smart, political, young black American would they look me up. It's a form of risk aversion and it's very boring. So I came home and did some more Shakespeare.

Realism

The audience suspend their disbelief more in the theatre than in front of a screen. On stage you can therefore get past the surface traits of height, accent, age, and so on, as long as the emotional core of the work is true. I can play Rosalind even though I'm a man; I can play Henry V even though he was Caucasian.

On the other hand, as an audience member watching film or television, you can make believe that you are present at the scene, that the camera isn't actually there and that you are a fly on the wall watching people react and interact. Any anomalies that don't quite make absolute, real sense will therefore stick out at you.

Having said that, some of the best drama on television is nonrealistic drama. I'm talking about shows like *The Singing Detective, Sex and the City, Six*

Feet Under, Ally McBeal, and actually *Hustle* as well — shows where people break out into song in the middle of the scenes, shows that use slow motion, direct address, dream sequences, and so on. Even the most realistic films or TV shows make use of camera effects, jumps in time, etc. So the requirement that television be literally realistic is really only a knee-jerk reaction; it's what some people in the industry feel the audience will accept. These people will only ever move one step behind public awareness, as they continually try to pander to it.

Doing Everything

I don't want to limit myself to one particular genre or medium of performance. I want to be able to do anything: comedy, musical, Shakespeare, film, or television. I am a restless animal and my choices so far have reflected that. Even if I could make a good living doing nothing but theatre I would try to hold out for some screen work. The opposite is also true. If I could make my living doing nothing but screen work both here and abroad, I would have to include the theatre. I can't exist as an actor without doing plays. I'd get too soft.

The Hierarchy

I don't get offered many film roles straight away. I have to read for parts like everyone else. To get the best choices in the business you have to be among the most famous, highest paid film actors in the industry. The next rung on the ladder is to be among the most famous, highest paid TV stars; and then comes theatre. Film is at the top, then TV, then theatre. That's the way it filters down. If you are known for being a great theatre actor, you'll get offers mainly in theatre. If you are known for television, that helps you get theatre easily, and TV, and a bit of film. But if you are known for being a good film actor, you can do more or less anything in television or theatre.

Los Angeles

As for L.A. itself, it's an industry town, sprawling and vacuous, with no real centre. There are many more opportunities for work, the weather is fantastic, and coming from the U.K., the cost of living is very reasonable and the people are genuinely positive. But all that still would not make me wish to leave home. It's safe to say that most people who have any degree of talent in the entertainment industry — be it in music, art, acting, directing, what have you — will aim for America and the West Coast because that is the seat of the industry. You get talented people from all over the world aiming for that one place. It has become such an incredible hotbed of talent that it's simply not true to say talent will out. The competition is just too strong. So I suppose I'm also saying that I would rather stay where I have managed to build up a reputation and a track record than move to a city where I could get lost in a crowd made up of some good actors and directors, but mainly of good-looking wannabes.

13
Peter Hall

Sir Peter Hall created the Royal Shakespeare Company in 1960. He was subsequently director of the National Theatre for fifteen years and opened the new South Bank complex. In 1999 and 2001, he directed three Shakespeare plays at the Mark Taper Forum in Los Angeles. At the time of this interview in September of 2001, he was rehearsing Otello *at the Lyric Opera in Chicago. Though Sir Peter is in his seventies, his international directing career — including both plays and operas — continues unabated.*

Theatre in L.A.

Directing in L.A. has really been very stimulating and interesting. And the audience is there. Of the three things I've done there so far, the most extraordinary was *Measure for Measure*. It played in the Ahmanson Theatre, which is a huge theatre. And clearly the audiences, twelve to fifteen hundred people, didn't know the play and didn't know what was going to happen next. And, frankly, with Clinton in the White House and Monica Lewinsky high in their minds, they were on the edge of their seats. Good for Shakespeare! He always tends to be topical.

There's a very good audience in L.A., and there's a lot of theatre in L.A. I think there will be more and I think it will get better. But I think Hollywood, Los Angeles, is a peculiar place. I remember the first time I went there in the '50s, I didn't know where the center was. They're developing a center now. They've got a new concert hall, the music center; they've remodeled the opera house. But Hollywood and West Hollywood and Beverly Hills don't want to trek down all the way downtown unless Placido Domingo is singing.

There is a huge amount of theatre going on, and there is a concentration of talent, acting talent, which is enormous. And thanks to one or two determined and dogged people in town, like Gordon Davidson at the Mark Taper, theatre has gradually increased. There was almost nothing there in theatre terms in the '50s when I went there, except pre-Broadway or post-Broadway tours. Now there's a ferment of activity — some good, some bad. And I think, just as people want museums, just as they want symphony concerts, just as they want live music, they also want live theatre. And more and more they'll want it.

Hollywood

Why has the world become colonized by American culture? Hollywood. It's a hundred years of Hollywood. Why are Coca Cola and McDonalds and American popular music found the world over? Hollywood. It's been the greatest empire builder in history that didn't have a sword. I don't think that's bad at all. Because I think wonderful things, wonderful films have come out of it.

But things have changed. Hollywood used to be dominated by showmen. They may have come up from fairgrounds and circuses and traveling theatre troupes, but they were showmen. They were tuned in to what excited the public. And I think now it's dominated by accountants who are led by balance sheets. I mean, obviously it's a commercial enterprise. But it doesn't make much sense as a business. If you really want to frighten a businessman, take him through the costs of a Hollywood movie and where the money went.

The thing I never understand about the stupidity of Hollywood is that they work on an actuarial basis: if you've made a successful movie, they must have you in their new movie because you're successful. But, from an actuarial point of view, if you've just had a success, you're still quite likely not to have a success next. I mean, all of us have failures. But Hollywood resolutely pretends there's no such thing as failure until it happens. You may be the most brilliant actor, but you make a lousy film — which is not your fault because the director screws it up or the studio takes it away from the director and recuts it — and then you're no longer hot. And then they don't hire you again. So they wreck talent, unfortunately.

Actor Crossover

I think it's just as hard to be a great movie actor as it is to be a great stage actor. A movie actor has to internalize it and make the camera come and look for it, and not go out and bully the camera. Whereas in the theatre you have to tell the audience, "I am very upset here"; you have to have a narrative quality of communication, which, if you do it badly, looks like overacting. If you do it well, it's sublime.

The television series or the movie career is clearly more important today than it was for the previous generation that I grew up and worked with. As an actor, if you don't have the draw power, you won't get the parts you want to do. And you won't get the draw power from the theatre unless you've done television and movies. If you don't do both, you may end up doing neither. It's a delicate balance, very delicate.

In London, there's still a tradition that you work on the stage, that you hone your craft on the stage, and that stage is important. There are quite a lot of actors in America who've never been on the stage. Of course, it's much easier to move from movies to stage in London.

You can say, "People only go to see plays that have a movie star in them." Well, yeah, but they go and see the plays. Provided the movie star can do it, I don't mind that. The economic problem is the main thing: the producers want the guarantee of the star. But there are very few stars that actually are a guarantee. Even with a star, it has to be good; it has to be an event. And certainly there are fewer stage stars in London than there were, but there are more wonderful actors.

Some say that if a movie star does theatre, it's because his career is languishing. I don't believe that. I directed Dustin Hoffman's Shylock. His career wasn't languishing. He gave me eleven months of his life.

I'm going back to London next to work on a play with Judi Dench, and Judi Dench is one of the two actors who really sell tickets. The other is Maggie Smith. There are no men, interestingly. America only discovered Judi Dench about five years ago. The first time I asked American Equity if I could bring a play to Broadway with Judi Dench in it, they said, "Judy who?" because they only give permission for stars. And that is one of the problems here, that the union is star-bent, not just the producers. They don't believe in talent; they believe in stars. It's an American thing. Very dangerous.

Broadway

I think Broadway is on the decline. Broadway is now a tourist attraction with plastic musicals that run forever. They don't do plays on Broadway. I went to Broadway first in 1957, and in those days the season started in September and closed more or less at the end of June when it got too hot. And that was the time when you did plays. And there were medium successes, there was obviously a hit here and there, and there were some flops, but there was a broad band. Since they invented the Tonys, that broad band has disappeared. No one will put a play on now before Christmas. Everybody puts plays on in March and April, and only one wins the Tony, and that's the one that runs and all the rest come off. So I think they've wrecked it.

Something's going to happen in New York. It has to. Because I think Off-Broadway is very turbulent and full of vitality and energy and things happening — if they ever get themselves around to being able to pay artists a living wage of some kind. There's plenty of theatre in New York, plenty of plays. The thing that always amazes me about New York, though, is that you can hear the best music, the best opera, see the best ballet, see the best art galleries in the world, but if you want to see Ibsen, Chekhov, Shakespeare, Molière, you have a hard time. There is no classical theatre tradition at all. And that's not Hollywood's fault; it's Broadway's fault.

Bad Theatre

A few months ago I sat in New York at The Producers, which is the most riotous, Aristophanic, bad-taste, extraordinarily life-enhancing thing you've ever seen in your life. And there were two thousand people alight, alight! Now that's theatre. That's good. It's got to be an event. It's got to be special. It's got to be tonight and for you only; you've got to feel personally privileged and excited to be there.

But if you just drifted in and there are three other people and there are a lot of bored actors — I mean, please. We are embarrassed for actors being bad in a bad play if they're live. We're not embarrassed when we see them in a movie. One can laugh at and be quite entertained by a really bad movie. We just think, "I hope they got paid a lot." But a really bad play makes you want to leave and leave fast. It's to do with the communal sharing. I don't want to be part of this; it's embarrassing to sit here with these people seeing that awful play and that awful performance. Instead of a bonding, there's a shrinking. And the result is you downgrade your audience's hunger for theatre and their liking of theatre and their participation in theatre.

The trouble about theatre is that too much of it — because of economic reasons, and social reasons, in what I think is an age of transition — is bad. And then people think theatre doesn't work. We have to admit, don't we, that there's a lot of bad theatre. There's more bad theatre than bad movies. There are plenty of mediocre movies. There's not much mediocre theatre; it's either bad or it's very good. But very good is very rare. And why is it very rare? Because it's very hard to do.

Audiences

You certainly have to work harder when you go into the theatre. A film tells you where to look. It dominates you. That's why you can't make a horror play. In the theatre, you do your own shots, your own cutting; you look from there to there to there. But the terror of sitting in the cinema and knowing that we might suddenly have a close-up of BLEEEAAH. We can't control it, we can't get away from it, all we can do is shut our eyes.

People complain about audiences. I think in my lifetime audiences have become more discriminating, sharper, more demanding, and, after all, they have become, certainly in England, bigger. Serious theatre — theatre that has integrity of purpose — I don't think is on the decline at all.

It also seems to me that television makes us better informed than we've ever been. (I'm talking about the positives now.) It seems to me that cinema makes available to an entire country performances by great actors that they otherwise would not have seen.

It's true we are a visual society and the attention span is less. But education on the whole is better. And I don't think audiences have ever been well-mannered. I don't think they were very well-mannered for Shakespeare. And they certainly weren't very well-mannered in the eighteenth or nineteenth centuries. After all, who chucked a dead cow on the stage at Macready in New York? I don't blame them. I don't think they should stay away if it's bad; they should come and shout and boo and stamp and rage and then come back and see if it has improved. I don't believe that audiences should be well-mannered. I really don't.

Of course, there is something about this bonding of the theatre audience. If people talk in the cinema, it's irritating, but it has no effect whatsoever on the performance. If people talk in the theatre, it breaks the bond. It's absolutely intolerable. Another example: if you go and see a movie and there's no one in the movie house, it doesn't matter. You stretch out your legs, you eat your popcorn, you enjoy the movie. But if you go to the theatre and there's no one in the theatre, you can't have the experience and you wish you hadn't come. It's the community imagining. Theatre makes people more intelligent collectively than they are individually. Absolutely. If I took a difficult speech of Shakespeare's and gave it to somebody and said, "Read it once and tell me what it means," not many people who weren't expert in the matter would be able to do it. But that same person sitting in the theatre — if the actor understands it — will understand it because of the collective sharing. We're a pack animal, we are a tribal animal; we operate collectively. We dance together, we sing together, we cook together.

One of the interesting things is that just as mass production has reduced skills in the individual, so mass production of entertainment has reduced the community spirit. I would predict that in this next century, live entertainment — whether it be music or theatre or opera — will all become more and more special and more and more valued. I think it will increase because it is a life-enhancing experience. It is neither better nor worse than screen, but totally different.

Essential Differences

You're talking to somebody who, in one month in 1957, was offered a training directorship at MGM in Hollywood and at the Stratford-on-Avon Festival. And I chose Stratford. That's how I got to form the Royal Shakespeare Company. I don't regret it. Theatre was always really my passion. I love movies and we live in a movie culture, and I've made one or two movies and I loved doing it. But if you put me up against the wall and said, "You've got to choose one or the other," I'd say theatre.

But the thing that interests me about film, what distinguishes it from theatre, is that it captures what happens at this second forever. I made a film called *Akenfield* in Suffolk about the country I was born in. I made it working weekends with real people and they improvised on a situation. They weren't actors. I could do that because I was able to shoot what they said at that particular moment. They never said it again, and I couldn't ask them to say it again. That seems to be one of the defining things about film, for me, anyway. I loved that experience.

What distinguishes theatre, on the other hand, is that it is a live imagining instrument in our community. Film doesn't make us imagine. Film has already done the imagining, and film says, "What you're looking at, *is*." Whereas theatre says, "Will you imagine … " Even in a room as small as this, if we put two rows of chairs there, cleared this out, and two very good actors came in and played a scene from *Julius Caesar* right there — if they were good enough — the people in these chairs would believe that this is Rome.

But if you put a camera there, and then showed what the camera has taken, our first reaction will be that they're in a modern room, they're not in Rome. "What are they talking about. Where's Rome?" In film, you can't have someone come on and say, "Will you imagine this is Agincourt." We will say, "No! Don't you have enough money to make Agincourt? Where's Agincourt?" Whereas in the theatre, if the actors are good enough and the text is good enough, we'll say, "Yeah, alright. And …?" You can say this sofa is the Rocky Mountains and we're going to climb over it because the essence of theatre is play and imagining.

Years ago I did the Monteverdi opera, *Il Ritorno di Ulisse in Patria*. Minerva is hovering above Ulysses, protecting him on his journey home. She's in full armor flying above him — breastplate, etc. When he reaches Ithaca, she descends and, in the space of one bar, turns into a shepherd boy. I can do that in a movie — a cut, dissolve, something like that. But how do you do it in the theatre? I had a really brilliant designer called John Bury — he's dead now, alas — and he designed a little tiny platform with a cloud and a rod, and on that rod was attached a breast plate and a helmet and a spear. When she stood behind it, she looked absolutely as if she were dressed in it. Then she descended to the floor and walked out of it. And every night the audience gasped. That's theatre. They could see how it was done, they knew how it was done, but it was exciting anyway.

You couldn't do that in a movie. You'd say, "That's silly," wouldn't you? You can't do that in film because film is not about the living moment. Film is dead — or anyway, it's a pretense. The film is twenty-four frames per second going through a projector, showing images which pretend to be a room. But they're not. They're abstract marks on a piece of celluloid. So the imagining is done. And we can't say, "Although that is a room on the screen, actually it's the Rocky Mountains." Film is looking at something which is already abstracted. And the abstraction, the formalization, has already happened by the making of the film. We believe that what we see actually was, even if it's a set in a studio. We *believe* it's real, whereas in the theatre, we *imagine* it's real. That's different. That's totally different.

I myself find theatre more thrilling and more engaging than film because it more readily takes on a metaphorical power which transcends what it is. Film can, and film does, of course. *Citizen Kane* is a great metaphorical picture that transcends its period and even transcends its fable. The other day I saw again the full version of *Apocalypse Now*. That transcends the Vietnam war. That is a metaphorical picture, going beyond itself. I imagine, I'm stirred. But film often gets stuck in naturalism.

Theatre used to be that way too. When I came into the theatre fifty years ago, if you were doing a scene with a dinner party, you would have to have the room and all the details, pictures on the walls, curtains on the window, all dressed and propped, because naturalism was what was expected in the theatre. And fifty years before that, the coming of naturalism was revolutionary.

If somebody opened the curtains and light flooded the room, that was an extraordinary event because, until that time, they hadn't had rooms in the theatre, or windows, and certainly no curtains. It was all painted on cloths in the eighteenth-century theatre. So, in Ibsen, the symbolic effect of those stage directions, letting light in, was very strong. But it's very hard for us to get that effect now because, in any film or television show we see, people open the curtain and the light comes in. Now we get our naturalism in the cinema.

So film has made theatre revalue what it is. You don't need to be naturalistic on the stage anymore. Now in the theatre you can show the lights, you can have a table and chairs, no plates, and the actors can actually mime, providing they're good enough actors, and the audience will say, "Well, that's a dinner party." If I filmed that, it would appear unacceptable, but in living terms, it's acceptable. It's the once-upon-a-time quality that theatre has. And audiences will also put short scenes together with a jump cut and a change of light just as they will in the movie house. If someone living in 1920 saw a modern movie, they wouldn't understand it; the grammar is completely different. But we're brought up on that grammar from childhood on, and that has affected the theatre. It certainly affected the nature of even Brecht's writing, even way back then. Most modern dramatists have a fluidity; they're not encompassed by having to have an interior and a maid coming on saying, "The master will be home soon." We don't care about that anymore. The cinema has freed us in the theatre.

In economic terms, they say there's a base inflation rate and then there's the inflation rate. And the base development rate of theatre over the last fifty years has been slowly up, in terms of quality, in terms of interest, and in asserting what it does that no other medium can do. That's the important thing.

14
Patrick Marber

Patrick Marber is a British playwright, screenwriter, and occasional theatre and television director. His plays include Dealer's Choice, Closer, Howard Katz, *and* After Miss Julie. *He wrote the screenplay for the film version of* Closer, *directed by Mike Nichols and starring Jude Law, Clive Owen, Natalie Portman, and Julia Roberts. This interview was conducted in the spring of 2002.*

Doing Both

What I really am is a playwright — a playwright who does screenplays as well, but really I'm a playwright. If I had to give up one, I'd give up the screenwriting.

I do screenplays for the pleasure of writing them, but also because it's necessary. I can't make a living as a playwright. Not quite. I mean, if every play I wrote was a hit, then, yeah, I could make a living. My last play wasn't a hit, so I have to write movies. I'm not complaining. There are worse things I could be doing to bring home the bread.

I decided that this year was the year I'd write two or three screenplays. That was a decision I made because I thought, "Well, I'm 37, and I've been offered movies for the last six or seven years. I've always turned them down for no apparent reason." Maybe I just couldn't be bothered, or maybe I didn't want to get involved; I just wanted an easy life. And then I started to think, "Well, I'm going to see if I can actually do it. Maybe my decision not to do movies was actually born of fear."

So now I'm taking it very seriously as a craft because I'm being offered them, and being offered them by people who are interesting to work with, and therefore it doesn't feel like a compromise to be writing for the movies; it actually feels very exciting. And it's fun to start learning something new.

It's fun; it's interesting work. I think screenwriting will affect my plays for the good. All writing is good for writing. Just writing my diary every now and then improves me as a writer. The job is to express something in words. Whatever discipline you're working in, it's always the same struggle, whether it's a play or a little thank you note to someone I've had dinner with. I take care on a thank you note; it upsets me if the words sound bad … he said, badly.

I'd like to feel that the same pen has written the play as has written the screenplay. I'd like people who know my work to say, "Ah yes, that's a Marber line, that's a Marber scene." I'm hoping for a particular sensibility, a certain wit — dare I say it — that's always at work whether I'm writing an article in the newspaper or a poem or a children's story or whatever. You want to have your own thing. I'm gently getting to my own thing over the years.

I direct plays, I've directed a bit of television, I write plays, I'm writing movies. It doesn't feel so different. It's not like I'm also trying to design furniture. I don't think it's any different from a writer who writes short stories, poetry, and novels. And lots of them do that. It's a much bigger leap to write poetry and novels than it is to write plays and screenplays. I'm not a polymath here; I'm just a hack trying to make a living.

Different Vocabularies

There are certainly differences. I think that film tends to be cutting to the chase. It depends on what kind of film you're in, of course, but even writing at the more "literary" end of the mainstream, the discipline is to keep telling [the] story and feeding the audience information and keep it exciting and peppy and moving along.

I happen to like a lot of dialogue in movies, if it's good dialogue, but I'm still seeing it primarily in terms of pictures. Writing a movie, I'm thinking, "Okay, that picture. Now I'm going to cut to that picture." I'm going to try to tell the story in the cuts as much as anything. I don't want the dialogue to convey the plot too much. Whereas when I write a play, I'm seeing two or three people talking. I'm telling the story in dialogue and that's where the emotional life of the story is.

On the stage you have the human voice and the human body, but the face isn't in close-up. On camera, the human face is as expressive as the word. The second you've got the opportunity of the face in close-up, you don't need so many words. The critic David Thomson said something wonderful, and I paraphrase: "The greatest special effect is the human face changing its mind."

Directing

I directed my adaptation of *Miss Julie* on TV. I really enjoyed that. Of all the things I've done, I think it's the most fully realized in terms of the three actors I had, the ability to edit it and control it as the director. It's absolutely what I'd imagined. It's the nearest I've got to achieving what I set out to do. Whether it's a success or not, I don't know; but it's what I wanted to do.

I've directed the premieres of all three of my stage plays. I didn't quite get what I wanted, but I was proud of what I did get and I loved working with the actors. Those productions might not have been definitive (I'm not sure any production is), but I think, "Yeah, to the best of our abilities, we delivered what we were able to deliver." But, as a playwright, you always have the dream that this genius director is going to come along and make your play better than it is. They're going to find stuff in it you didn't know was there. They're going to do this beautiful production. They're going to have the finest actors that ever lived.

I've had a little of that experience, actually. I've seen productions of plays of mine abroad, in Sweden and Germany, where they rehearse for three or four months. They really dig deep. They've got money, and they take the theatre very seriously. America prides itself [*doing American accent*]: "Oh, the *theatre!* We *love* the theatre." Well, yes, but go to Sweden, where they've got actors who've been working together in a company for ten years! The understanding between them, and the lack of ego, and the quality and integrity of their work — it's magnificent. It's a totally different universe, and the standard is so high, I think, because they're not wholly concerned with commerce.

Here in England it's pretty commercially minded. We don't have long rehearsal times — maybe four or five weeks for the West End. At the National Theatre, you get six, seven, maybe eight weeks rehearsal time, which often makes a huge difference to the work.

Sam Mendes insisted on rehearsal time for *American Beauty*. I think film directors who have come from the theatre tend to demand it. If they have the power to get it in their contracts, they will. I can't imagine how others do it without rehearsal, but they do. Many a great movie has been made without it.

But I am surprised that some actors can go through their whole careers and do very little on stage. The stage is your only opportunity as an actor to be in full control of your performances — to modulate it and change it and really explore it. On film, you're at the mercy and whim of a director with whom you may or may not agree. The director can use five different takes to construct one two-line speech. I've done it myself as a TV director. You're absolutely in control of what performance the actor is giving. You can make them do anything. You can make them give a longer pause than they gave; you can steal a smile from another take and put it in. The power is unbelievable. Film actors have to put a lot of trust in their directors. It must be very painful sometimes watching the results and thinking, "But that's not the performance I gave!"

A film actor has a completely different process, a completely different perspective, from the director's. For the actor, it's got to feel real, it's got to feel right. But a film director might be thinking, "Screw your process. I just want this moment. I don't care if you fake it, as long as it looks real." Because, quite rightly, the director is a whore trying to get the shot before the light goes. Often for the director, "It looks right, it sounds right, forget about it." Not so for the poor actor.

Status

As a writer in film, in general, you're a second-class citizen. Well, actually, at the beginning you're God, because you're the only person working on the project, apart from the studio execs. They've bought a book, they've hired a writer, and you're going to write this film. And you *are* the project, so you get a lot of attention, they treat you very well. It's a great big love-in.

But the second you deliver, you're a second-class citizen, you're a slave, you're a minion, you're this schmuck. You've screwed up this wonderful book they bought — or maybe not, maybe they'll love it. Either way, as soon as it's with them, it's their beast to rip to pieces as they see fit. I don't own the material anymore; they can do whatever they want with it. And they will. I've had that experience. I wrote a script two years ago which the studio hated. They said, "Oh, it's too faithful to the book"; whereas in the meetings it had been, "We all love this book, so let's be true to it." So I wrote very faithfully to the book. "Egh, we hate it. Too dark. Too faithful to the book. Put the book on the shelf," was the phrase. And I said, "I'm not prepared to put the book on the shelf because I really like the book." And they got various other writers, including a very famous writer. Screenplay after screenplay gets written of this book. Execs come and execs go. And now, two years later, a new exec has come back to my script. "Well, actually, it's quite good. I think we're going to make it." I'll find out over the next week whether they are.

So nothing is surprising to the writer in Hollywood. I'm just glad I don't have to go there to make a living. If that was how I made my living solely, by living in L.A., right in the beast, writing movies for a living, I'd go insane. There are many perfectly good writers whose work never gets made. And they're just sitting there in their big houses with lots of money and they've never had a screenplay made because they're in permanent turnaround.

In the theatre, the playwright is top of the tree, first-class citizen; has the right to approve director, cast; gets involved in rehearsals (if you pick a decent director who's interested in the writer's opinion); people know you wrote the play — unless it's got big stars in it and a star director. But in general the playwright is respected, certainly in England. That's true in the States too. I think the playwright is absolutely valued in the States … as long as he's got a hit, and doesn't forget it.

Of course, the laughter is great. And the applause is great. But, as the playwright, when the audience applauds, you don't think they're applauding you; they're applauding the actors. I did a bit of acting a few years ago — I was in Mamet's *Speed the Plow* in the West End — and that's much more of an ego trip than being a playwright. You stand there, you bow, they're clapping. That's great. Actors get much more. They have a tough life because they get a lot of rejection, but that applause is much better for the ego. As a playwright, there's a lot of failure, too. You're endlessly trying to believe in yourself, often with no apparent evidence. I was talking to Harold Pinter literally a week ago — he is, in my view, the greatest living playwright — and he said, "This is a tough business." He still thinks it's a tough business, and he's going to be performed forever.

Glamour

I like the atmosphere backstage. I like going in the stage door rather than the front door. It's just fun to be behind the scenes. I like the camaraderie, I like the jokes. I like the tradition very much — that you're part of something that's been going for a very long time, and that you can stand on a stage in London and say, "Olivier stood here. Coward stood here. Oscar Wilde saw the premiere of his play in this theatre. John Osborne was here." That's a fantastic thing. You're carrying the torch. It's glamorous, romantic. So I like all those things. And I really like not having to get up in the morning and go to an office. I like being able to sit in my pajamas and do my job. What greater privilege is there? So I like all the extracurricular elements of the job. And then I guess I like expressing myself in words. I just always wanted to be a writer, and here I am.

Theatre is a ritual. It was always a ritual. Film has been around only a hundred years. Theatre is sacred, from the Greeks onward. In the theatre you can say, "I was there." The difference between going up the Eiffel tower and seeing a postcard of it, maybe. "Yeah, I was there. I saw Harold Pinter on stage, acting in one of his plays."

Rarely Perfect

I've had as good emotional and aesthetic experiences in movies as I have in theatre. Absolutely. The first time I saw *Taxi Driver* or *Raging Bull* or *The Godfather* or *Apocalypse Now, All About Eve, Citizen Kane*. Great masterpieces.

And then there are novels. Reading Philip Roths' *Sabbath's Theatre* was as good an experience as anything I've had in any theatre. If we're going to talk about genres, I don't think you can beat the novel, really, in terms of pure aesthetic pleasure — to be transported by a masterpiece of literature, to really work your imagination. I think the novel is way ahead, I'm afraid — much more powerful. To read *Lolita* for the first time and find yourself gripped by this amazing story, this amazing prose. Because you're experiencing unremitting genius; whereas in the theatre, it's very rarely perfect: "Well, the servant wasn't so good and so-and-so was inaudible in that big speech in Act II." With *Lolita,* it's all Nabokov there; it's concentrated genius.

Devaluing Language

I don't think you can say that theatre is exclusively language based. My kind of theatre is. But there are a lot of people out there who would say, "What's wrong with the theatre is that it's language based. And this has been its problem from the year dot." I happen to disagree with those people. But that's another matter. For me, the theatre is about actors and words.

But the word is devalued in our culture. People say it's because we have a generation who don't read books. But I just don't think that's true. I think the word is devalued because you've got people like George Bush as president. I'm serious! If you have someone as the president of the most powerful country in the world who can't use language, what kind of example is that? If a political figure emerged who could talk, and talk beautifully and brilliantly and inspiringly, they'd get on in politics. But the talented people don't want to go into politics because they get murdered by the media and it's a terrible life and they'd rather be in movies. The idea of rhetoric, that beautiful idea that you can be taught rhetoric, maybe it'll come back. I'd sign up for the classes.

Show Business

I think there are as many talented people working in the movies as there are in the theatre. Theatre isn't necessarily better or more artistic; there's a lot of terrible, stodgy rubbish out there. There are usually ten good stage productions a year, and there are usually ten good movies a year.

Of course, you're much more conscious in the movie world that you're in a business and that it's a money-making business. Hollywood is one extreme of the "entertainment industry"; that's a given, and you'd be a fool to think otherwise. If it will make money, they'll make it; it's really that simple, and why shouldn't it be? The art house sector has exactly the same concerns: "Are we going to get our money back?" And there are artists who can work within that, who can convince people that this film will make money, and stick to their guns and have final cut, and they achieve it. And impressively so.

In the theatre, you're much less conscious of the commercial imperatives. They're still there, they're just not spoken of, certainly in the subsidized English theatre; it's considered a bit vulgar. In London, I have no idea what my plays have taken, grossed, what's the percentage — I have no idea. Whereas working on Broadway, you're very conscious of the money, of the grosses, "the wrap." The wrap is God in the Broadway theatre. I didn't know what "the wrap" was when I arrived in New York. By the time I left, "The wrap, what's the wrap?" "What did we wrap today?" "What did we wrap this week?" — because the wrap is absolutely indicative of whether my play is going to be on next week. And you learn that. I knew every single week what the box office was doing.

But I didn't mind, particularly. Those were just the rules. And if I didn't like the rules, I could have put *Closer* on Off-Broadway and had an easier life. But I wanted in my lifetime to have a play on Broadway, and I thought, "Well, how many times am I going to have a hit? This is my shot." So I took it. I'm glad I did. It was fun, and even when it wasn't fun, it was interesting.

I felt on Broadway, "I'm in show business here." I knew that. I wanted that experience. You don't feel that when you've got a show on in the West End. You're in showbiz, but who cares. Whereas on Broadway, people talk about the theatre in restaurants, in the newspapers, on the TV. To be nominated for a Tony in New York is a big deal; it means something, albeit briefly.

I don't think Shakespeare would have thought about art versus entertainment. "Am I an artist, am I an entertainer?" Not a concern. But those were concerns I had years ago. Now, I find it so hard to write anything, I just get on with it. It's a phase of youth. It's not that I've grown out of it; of course I want to be an artist. That would be nice. But my primary concern is with the material in hand. I thought a lot more about art versus entertainment when I wasn't writing — when I was a wannabe. "Oh, what am I doing?" Well, I wasn't doing anything. Now I'm too busy to dwell on these matters.

Audiences and the Avant-Garde

As a playwright, I tend to cut to the chase. I think it comes from having done stand-up comedy, where you're so conscious of the audience and whether they're paying attention, whether they're going to throw things, whether they're laughing. The only sound you want to hear as a comic is laughter; you're not interested in silence. You'll do anything to avoid silence. That's your job. Whereas, as a playwright, I see my job as being to control silence. It's a new craft for me. And when I first started writing plays — young playwright, not entirely confident — my plays were full of the paranoia that the audience might get bored. This is something *I* know; I don't think an audience would feel that necessarily. But I'm now beginning to relax a little and allow myself a bit more time in a play, and to trust that my dialogue will hold the audience's attention even if it's slow. With my third play I was less worried.

In the theatre, I do think there are some people who really don't care if there's an audience, and I don't care for them much. I believe they're known as "the cutting edge" or avant-garde. Who knows? Maybe there was an avant-garde in Shakespeare's time and we just don't get to hear about them. They must have been terrible [*resisting the temptation to do an impression of an Elizabethan avant-garde performance artist*] — mummers jerking around in the countryside, thinking they were bringing art to the people. They'd have been there. Take Shakespeare — at the time, established author, establishment author. There must have been some guys who thought he was a shmuck, a no-talent, he lucked in, and *they* were writing the real plays but they couldn't get them on; they were doing private readings in barns! There must have been an angry section who weren't getting a look-in. Of course. There always is. But we don't hear about them because history is written by the winners, as we know. There might be a sitcom here. …

Tom Stoppard said in an interview, "There are very few undiscovered masterpieces out there in any media in any form." Very, very few. Because the world is hungry for art. That's my optimistic view. Certainly that's true in the mainstream, and we're talking about the mainstream and I'm in the mainstream — or, rather, the tributaries that feed it. Mamet said (and I paraphrase heinously), "Listen to the way people talk about a performance artist and listen to the way people talk about Cary Grant, and that's all you need to know about the avant-garde." I kind of agree. I'm not necessarily against the avant-garde. I just know I'm not of it.

The Future

People do go to the theatre. I'm not pessimistic. They're still going. They go to my plays, bless them. All the good plays in London are full. Harold Pinter is on at the National Theatre with *No Man's Land. Private Lives* is on in the West End playing to a thousand people a night. It's great. There's stuff out there and people are going to it. If it's good, the people will come. That's my optimistic belief. I'm one of them; I'm a punter, I'm a fan, I'm a theatre-goer. I want to see good stuff.

A lot of it's to do with marketing, and stars and all that. It's wide open for someone to come along and go, "Okay, we're going to market this aggressively, interestingly, originally." Drew Hodges, who marketed *Closer* on Broadway, is one of the people who thinks this way. He's a really smart guy. If I were a businessman, I'd open a theatre marketing company. I'd start one of those off.

But theatre will carry on as it always has. There will always be some good stuff sitting atop the bad. And it will always be too expensive. The theatre would have a healthier, better, and brighter future if they reduced ticket prices, and I hear that is what Nick Hytner intends to do at the National. But theatre will carry on because human beings gathering in a place to watch other human beings doing something seems to be necessary — be it sports, theatre, opera, church, a wedding, a funeral. This is the stuff of human life; we need to watch each other.

15
Drew Hodges

Drew Hodges is the founder and principal/creative director of SpotCo, an advertising agency that has handled numerous Broadway shows, including Rent, Chicago, The Vagina Monologues, Long Day's Journey into Night, *and* Avenue Q. *He gave this interview in January of 2001.*

The Uses of Celebrity

Because all Broadway shows are miked, anyone can be in a show. And that is not necessarily a bad thing. Rosie O'Donnell went into *Seussical* last night. She doesn't have a singing voice. She doesn't have a studied voice. That's just not who she is. But Rosie has been a huge lift for that show.

A lot of us really love *Seussical.* It's been one of my favorite things to work on. And it's been really tough to watch it get slammed because of this press juggernaut thing that happened to it. And while I'm sure that some of these critics genuinely don't like it, it really was set up for a fall. Audiences will react to what they're told; you can have a show that got good laughs the night before, then the review will say this is howlingly funny, and the next night the laughs will get much bigger — or, vice versa, they'll tone down for a while because people react to their expectations. We all know that, and I've worked on things that got poor reviews before where the producers tried to convince themselves that people liked it better than they did. But *Seussical* is a show that people really, sincerely love. I can tell you, I've been in there — people are really enjoying this show. So we have just been waiting out the negativity from the reviews.

And then, last night, Rosie's first night, was like opening night. People were screaming, yelling, rushing the aisles. My friend Kevin Chamberlin is in the cast playing Horton the Elephant, and he said he felt this incredible lift from the audience. This audience was not affected by reviews, and the result was that we got back this much purer audience. It was really moving to watch these actors who have had a pretty tough run — being battered about and directors coming and going, everyone really struggling to make this thing work — suddenly get back this total enthusiasm from an audience that's really lifting them and giving them such a positive feeling.

And yes, I'm sure there is resentment about it when a TV personality comes in and steals the show from professional actors, but actors know how it goes. There's no fame like TV fame; not even movie fame is like TV fame. Stage actors used to have real fame, you know, national fame. But that was also when the pop chart was show tunes. And basically nowadays there's no easier way than TV for someone to be famous because they're in your house all the time. There's no going back from that; it's just based on familiarity. Someone you see every day in your house is someone you feel like you know. On a marketing level, there's nothing like consistency, repeating and repeating. You don't get that with stage actors — you don't really get to know Blair Brown or whomever. You see them in one show, and then there's time in-between. I think it's the rare person, the Nathan Lane, who is always on the stage.

Borrowing Mass Marketing Techniques

Theatre has generally not been marketed like other contemporary entertainments — records, movies, cable — and it is becoming this niche area primarily because it is being put forward that way, because it isn't defending itself as a mass entertainment against the others. The techniques of marketing a Broadway show often feel to me really behind the techniques that I use or see being used by other people around me for all these other mass media entertainments.

To avoid that here at my company, we don't let anyone get completely insulated by working just for theatre clients. We have this theory of high/low culture. We'll do something mass market like the *Survivor* logo and then something really refined like Theatre Complicité's new piece. We also try to use outside people — illustrators, photographers, writers, TV commercial directors — who have never done theatre before. You'll deal with mainstream people of great renown within their field, many of whom have never been asked to work on a theatre piece, and they'll respond immediately to it. It's an art form that everyone has a real warmth about. You can get people to do things that you wouldn't expect. And they bring to it a new energy, a new vitality, that the theatre needs.

What we're trying to do is apply to theatre the same branding ideas that you would apply to any contemporary entertainment. Successfully marketed films, for instance, always have a point of view as to who they are and who they're going after. And theatre is so easy to do that way because any successful production has a strong sense of its own personality. We're not specifically looking to market against a movie or a record; we're just trying to use the same techniques. For instance, we're always looking at the rest of the season, what environment the show is going into. But, at the same time, everyone is fighting for the same dollar. You can go this weekend to a Broadway show or a movie, and I think you might make a decision as to one or the other.

Reaching Outside the Core Audience

Probably the main difference in marketing films and plays is that a movie is being released by a studio that has a whole slate of movies, and the studio hopes that when one movie fails, another one wins. There's a larger picture. Whereas on any given show, that particular combination of people and money is there only once. So there really isn't the ability to put a ton of money out there and hope that if this one doesn't work, that other one will.

And since you never know if a show is going to work up-front, you're always working with the most conservative budget you possibly can, which creates a catch-22. Your most efficient buy is to reach out to the person most likely to go to your show; but if you don't reach out farther, you can't enlarge the audience who goes to theatre. Theatre is constantly trying to get new audiences, but it can't quite afford to get new audiences. And so theatre marketing tends to speak only to people who already go to the theatre.

The most successful campaigns get outside of that. For instance, we marketed *Rent* in a really rock-and-roll way. The advertising doesn't tell you what's going to happen; it tells you how it's going to feel to go. A lot of really good movie trailers are like that. With *Rent,* we had to address the problem that musicals are not hip. I'm not a hip guy. I'm a really mainstream kind of guy. But I was in those worlds when we did Swatch and MTV. That stuff was really hip; it was the hippest stuff — snowboarding, Keith Haring. So I know a lot of people from the hip, style world, and they feel that theatre is trite, overly emotional — particularly musicals. So when the *Rent* campaign started, I wrote this headline that said, "Don't you hate the word musical?" I definitely got some calls from people in the industry! But I hate it that people who I think would love this show instantly turn off and go, "Oh, I don't like musicals."

Our ads were in the subway. Just being in the subway was an amazing thing to do at that time, to be there with everybody and not just in the *New York Times* arts section. And we tried to write that whole campaign from a point of view that would make sense to someone on the subway. One of the panels was about how you buy tickets, because we didn't think that everybody in this age group knows where these tickets come from. So there was a line that said, "You can buy them at Ticketron, the same place you get your concert tickets." And it listed the prices, including these twenty-dollar seats in the first two rows. One of the things that happens in discussion about Broadway ticket prices is that everyone always names the top price. *Rent* has a really good thirty-five-dollar ticket; it's a small theatre and you can see great. No one ever talks about thirty-five dollars. So we wrote this thing that said, "Okay, there are tickets that are sixty-five dollars, this and this, for twenty dollars you have to work a little, you have to stand outside." And we wrote it in the plainest language we possibly could, to say, "This is what you need to know."

Making It Easier

Everybody I know who's a forward-thinker in the theatre would like to make the process easier. Disney did it and *Chicago* did it when lines were crazy: providing concierges who were going through the line saying, "What dates are you looking for?" and letting people know that they were already sold out on that date so prepare your second date before you get to the window. And also the web stuff. I don't understand why every ticket isn't sold on the web. It's a really good way to buy a theatre ticket. You can see exactly where you'll sit. You don't have a line of people behind you. And we are seeing web sales really going up. We have shows that have 15 and 20 percent of their sales on the web. That's a lot considering how long it takes people to get over the tradition of going and standing in the box office line.

Theatre has become a more special occasion thing than a daily thing. That's a function of price and location. Distribution is everything from a modern marketing point of view. Movies come to you, but you have to come to theatre. Of course, that's also part of what makes it special. Every theatre lover has a tale of coming to New York and walking around Broadway and the excitement of how that feels. It wouldn't be the same if it were just down on the corner.

But I think we still have to make it easier. Theatres don't always have comfortable seats; theatres don't always have great sight lines. This trend towards rebuilding the twenty-five-plexes, building those elaborate buildings, was originally taking a note from theatre; in order to compete with VCRs, they had to make the place you went to feel better than being in your own house. But that's an area where theatre is really behind now.

An Acquired Taste

We all talk about the kids sleeping overnight to see *Rent*. We tell our other clients, "You should be happy they're sleeping there because two years from now they'll be coming to your show." Theatre is an acquired taste.

I'll give you an example. The designers here are anywhere from twenty-two to thirty-two years old; they're pretty young. One of them comes from MTV, one of them comes from a record label; they're very hip. They're generally not theatre fanatics, and some of them are almost anti-theatre. They certainly weren't people who had gone to musicals. But now they all go because they're working on the shows. They don't always like it. We just sent two of the designers to the Lincoln Center Library to watch this videotape of *Oklahoma* and they totally didn't get it. But you also definitely see them learning theatre and beginning to say, "That was cool. I really liked that. That was interesting." It's like wine. You build a taste for wine, and maybe later on you get more sophisticated about why a great wine is great and how long it took and what it took to make that, but in the beginning you just have to like it.

16
Gordon Davidson

American director Gordon Davidson has been the artistic director of the Mark Taper Forum theatre in Los Angeles for thirty-eight years. This interview was conducted in the late summer of 2004, just before the launch of his final season before retirement.

Doing Theatre in L.A.

One of the best things about doing theatre here in L.A. is that there is this incredible pool of talent — not just actors, but directors, designers, sound technicians, composers, and, of course, writers. They're here because of film, but, in varying degrees, they have a hunger to do the stage. And of course the worst thing about doing theatre in L.A. is that very same condition, because those people — especially actors — are under pressure to keep themselves free for the next film opportunity. Either they need to for financial reasons or they're told that if they don't they'll lose their position in the hierarchy of desirable talent.

There are times when it's better, times when it's worse. I came out here in 1964 to assist John Houseman on a production of *King Lear* at The Theatre Group at UCLA, which was a professional theatre on the campus. It came together because of the pool of people here with stage history, including John. John split his life between film and theatre. He and a group of established artists like Robert Ryan and Eva Marie Saint founded the theatre in order to allow stage actors who had come to Hollywood a chance to continue their work on the stage. A wave of them came in the '50s and the early '60s when television series started to become significant. These were actors who had those stage muscles and didn't want them to go slack. It was not about being recognized in order to get the next job in film.

The thing that made The Theatre Group possible was the "hiatus," when the series stopped shooting for the year. Usually the hiatus would be three months in the late spring and early summer, and then the series would start up again in the fall. So, in those three months, you had these transplanted New York actors looking for stage work. That was the dynamic for The Theatre Group at that time — trying to take full advantage of the talent pool, but always keeping in mind that the reason for doing it was larger than the idea of Hollywood.

Now the landscape has changed. There still is a hiatus for sitcoms and series shows, but pilots have filled in that time, as well as movies for television. For a good working actor — the kind you want to cast — the year can easily be eaten up by a combination of series work, pilots, and two-hour movies for television.

And, of course, the other major change is cable. When I came out here, there were only the three networks plus PBS. The universe is not static and it never has been.

Forming a Company

I had a dream from the earliest days of forming a company. In my era, the idea of company was really strong. When you see a great company, you can see the difference. For example, Steppenwolf — though it is partly a victim of its own success — does put its own stamp on the work: there is a definite style, and people coming into the company absorb that.

My first job was with the American Shakespeare Festival Theater and Academy in Stratford, Connecticut. We had journeyman actors who played the servants — that was the "academy" part of it — and then wonderful veteran actors. A well-known, very experienced actress was playing the countess in *All's Well That Ends Well* and the guy playing the servant had part of a scene with her. As he was exiting after the scene, I watched her stop him and say, "Let me finish the line. Just look at me, and then go. That's how you'll get your laugh." No director could give more valuable input. I love that idea of senior actors teaching the craft, passing it on.

The English have held on to the idea of a resident company longer, but more and more I hear that even there actors are saying, "I can't commit for nine months. It's too hard." People are entitled to make a living — not a killing, just a living.

I realized very early on that it was not going to be possible to have a company here in L.A. because the pressure was just too great on the mature working actors. Jason Robards had become a friend of mine in the early days; he was in the first show in the Ahmanson. Way back in those early days I said, "Jason, what would it take to have you join a company? I'm just starting here and I'd like to know." He thought a moment and said, "Five hundred dollars a week." Perfect. But gone are the days.

One thing that tends to happen, in general, and maybe in particular here, is that a young company (just out of school) works for maybe ten years; then the members start to have families, they have to settle down, and it's harder to maintain that level of company-based work. So those things come and go, both by the age of the participants and the temper of the times.

And, of course, the differential has gotten even greater now between what you get paid as a stage actor and what you can get in television and the movies.

Base salaries have moved up in theatre, as have star salaries, but it's nowhere near the incredible deals that are available in film.

The Loss of Continuity

What I think is happening — a sad thing from my perspective — is the loss of continuity. I'm seeing a lot of young actors for the play I'm doing right now because I want that energy; but sometimes I'll say something like, "When Rosemary Harris played so-and so ...," and they'll say, "Who?" There are legendary stage actors they've just never heard of.

So the question is how to keep the continuity alive. You want each generation to see the previous generation. It doesn't take very long for a couple of new generations to come along who are completely cut off from the past.

Fame

I had a little taste of fame. I acted in an episode of *Will & Grace*. I was hired to play the part of a director, and I was directing James Earl Jones, who was the guest star. Surprisingly, his was a comic role. He was actually very funny. I was on screen for all of ten, maybe fifteen, seconds, but people came over to me in the shopping center and said, "Didn't I just see you on *Will & Grace?*" And that's the power of the medium.

Different Skills

I think there are many young actors who would like to believe that they are going to make a career primarily on the stage, but who find out — sooner than they used to in the past — that they can't do it. There are fewer plays being done, for one thing. Broadway isn't the place that it was. And then there are the challenges. Eight performances a week, five on the weekend if it's a Tuesday through Sunday schedule — the energy that takes, the vocal demands. Very different from film or television.

There are some actors who can do both, who don't have any trouble, but there are certainly some who can be very real and intense on film who just can't come across on stage. On stage, if I'm playing a scene with you, we both have to deal with the audience; they have to hear you, they have to feel you, they have to be involved (not necessarily in an obvious way). On a thrust stage like ours, the playing space is three-dimensional, so I have to push my voice out and behind and yet not feel that I'm shouting. The ability to include the audience and yet not play to them is essential. Physical stamina is a big issue. And there are actors who never get over the fear of acting in front of an audience; they're simply afraid they'll forget their lines.

We've had film actors work here who will sometimes have a hard time understanding why they have to do the scene the same way every time. Their training and the medium itself is so different. They're used to thinking, "If the take doesn't work, we'll do it again and we'll get one good one out of them." Not in the theatre.

And there's the question of sensitivity to the qualities of language, which also comes through training. I'm sure there are some film-trained actors who say, "What's the difference what I say?" or "I don't feel comfortable saying that." But more of them simply don't have the techniques to allow the text to do its work.

And then there's the question of size. When you're playing a scene for a movie, you don't have to do very much and it can still be electric. And I think actors tend to play it more safe in film. In the theatre, it's rewarding when someone is willing to go out on a limb. The consequence can be over the top, so that you don't believe a moment of it, but the best is a mix of the two — to have basic truth but also something primal and extraordinary, something larger than life.

I use this image. In the movie theatre, I think you'll see two people sitting here, two people sitting over there, and kind of slumping back in their seats. In the theatre there's a tendency to sit bunched together (of course we sell the tickets that way) and leaning forward. And that's mirrored by what the actors are doing — communicating with and including the audience in the journey of the play.

Raisin in the Sun

I went to see the new Broadway production of *Raisin in the Sun,* thinking, "Well, it's a nice play. ..." I went with some hesitation because I'd read the reviews and it was felt that Sean Combs didn't really deliver what was required of him for the role of Willie. But I went anyway, and what was eye-opening to me was how good the play was, how absolutely brilliant. It's not just a '50s play; it transcends time. It's very intelligent and insightful and contemporary. But it was a different play than expected because Willie is usually the center-piece, and Combs didn't have the craft, and you'd expect that would torpedo the whole thing. But somehow he supported the rest of the play. It was an amazing thing. And at the same time, he's a major star, so people came to see him and there were lines around the block at the stage door, and those who came were rewarded with this other gift that they didn't expect.

Commercial Pressures

I think filmmaking is an extraordinary art form that is no more driven by commercial success than a Broadway musical. Yes, if you put ten million dol-lars together to make something, you're damn well going to have to make it back. But there are certain pressures everywhere. Even if the box office covers only 50 percent of the cost of running this theatre, it's an important 50 percent.

I bargain with my board. Some of them feel that a play was a real flop if tickets didn't sell. And I have to keep saying, "That's not the reason we did it." But obviously, if you do too many plays like that you go out of business. So it's a tap dance: budget balance and content, vision and the freshness of the storytelling.

Theatre, Film, and Politics

Things don't stay static. They ebb and flow. When I came out here in '64, movies and television weren't dealing in any significant way with the political world we were living in: civil rights, women's lib, the '68 convention, the Vietnam War. And I felt very strongly that the theatre could and should be a voice in that dialogue. People sitting together in a dark room become a community, and the more that community reflects the real world, the more powerful it is politically. Which is, by the way, why I have always been very interested in diversity, both on the stage and in the seats.

But now there are plenty of movies — documentary, quasi-documentaries, great independent feature films — that deal with the world/global confrontations as well as our own political landscape. So what does that leave the theatre to do? In planning this last season, I would have loved to do a play about Iraq or the Middle East or the nature of politics in relationship to that, but I couldn't find that play, and I tried but couldn't make one satisfying enough. And it frustrated me. But as I gave up on that idea, I found myself gravitating to plays that were much more about the human heart, personal choices, relationships, the social conscience of individuals. Now there seems to be some kind of switch, so that when people come together in the theatre away from CNN, they need something less about politics and more about humanity.

A Better Time

If I were coming up now, I don't know whether I could have founded this theatre. I think I came along at the perfect time. Not that someone else can't make a future now, but I do think it's harder. There are so many distractions; theatre is not a staple of people's diet. There aren't enough good things happening. Not that people aren't trying. It's just that the hunger for theatre on the part of audiences has been deflected. Subscribers tell me they're not going to renew because traffic is too hard to deal with. Or both spouses are working and they're too tired to go out on a weeknight.

But I think there will always be theatre. It may have to be smaller, but there will always be two boards and a passion. That's the kind of theatre I like. I think I'll try it!

17
Linda Emond

American actor Linda Emond played leading roles in major Chicago theatres before moving to Los Angeles and then New York, where she is now based. Emond's television and film work includes appearances on The Sopranos, Law & Order, *and in Walter Salles's* Dark Water. *Her New York stage work includes a Tony-nominated performance as Inez in Yasmina Reza's* Life(x)3; *Elaine in Craig Lucas's* The Dying Gaul; *and her acclaimed performance as* The Homebody *in Tony Kushner's* Homebody/Kabul. *Emond worked closely with Kushner over a period of five years as he was developing the play. This interview was originally conducted in 2000 and was updated in the spring of 2005.*

Assumptions

The nature of celebrity and all that goes along with it (interviews, talk shows, gossip columns) makes actors' lives open season. There is a hunger for this information, and it gets ravenous at times. The amount that is written about actor-celebrities is overwhelming, isn't it? When there is so much out there publicly, it opens the door for all sorts of opinions and armchair psychology about us. And that leads to a lot of easy categorizing: "Oh, you're an actor. I know what that means." This is true in life in general, of course, but boy oh boy is it exaggerated here.

The received wisdom is that actors want to be famous; that they are fairly self-indulgent, self-centered beings who crave applause; that they see theatre as only a stepping stone to bigger things; that they anxiously await the reviews after opening night; that winning awards gives their lives meaning; etc. None of those things happens to be true for me, nor for most actors I know and work with. But, even among actor friends and others in this field, there is great disparity in how we respond. In the end, though, it's all pretty darn public. If I do one play versus another, there are assumptions about that. If I say I'm not going to do a play, there are assumptions about that. And, generally, these assumptions are in keeping with the bigger assumptions about what motivates me.

Why should I care that anyone else understand exactly what is important to me or why I make the choices I make? Obviously, it's only important that *I* stay in touch with why. I strive to stay grounded in the work I want to do, to make my own personal choices for my own reasons. But I admit that I do often have to *strive* to do that. It doesn't always come easily given the public nature of what I do.

And I am not famous at all. I can only imagine what life is like for Julia Roberts. Yikes. I've worked with some very famous people and it can get positively trippy. I worked with Al Pacino on a play a couple of years ago. He's a superstar! He walks into a restaurant and the chemistry changes in the room. Reality is immediately *altered*. And does he enjoy that? A lot of people do just fine with celebrity, but I think most of them — most of the sane ones, anyway — would say that it isn't something they enjoy; it's just the price they pay for making a good living and having a degree of artistic control.

Working in Chicago

There is something different about Chicago. Careers are not necessarily made or broken in Chicago. Careers *are* made and broken here in New York, and that can affect how people treat their work. You hear about actors' performances changing during the Tony voting period — becoming showier. And, of course, people will be more nervous because they feel there is so much more at stake. For better or worse, there is!

The shadows of Hollywood and stardom don't loom nearly so large in Chicago; it all seems very far away. There's so little celebrity there and such a strong non-equity scene, and some of that Midwestern work ethic is also very much a part of the theatre scene — all that creates an energy that supports everything else. It creates a straightforward, unglamorous, feet-on-the-ground, let-me-do-the-job-and-try-to-do-it-well kind of culture that's bred into the people who work there. It was the theatre environment I knew. And I'm so grateful for that because the experiences there taught me well.

I chose to go to Chicago because I saw it as a place where I could actually live and go to the theatre and work with a group of people and integrate the things I had learned in the intensive training program I'd just been through. And all of that was very true. I might very well still be there if I hadn't basically acted until I dropped. I was just working nonstop. One of my best pals told me that I'd lost my sense of humor and she was right. I was working overtime, barely making a living, very fatigued creatively, and I just couldn't see my way out of that cycle.

Disenchantment with the Work

That fatigue was very much a part of what led to a period of deep disenchantment about the state of American theatre. From my experiences, I came to think that the regional theatre movement in this country was a great benefit but also a great blow to the arts. A great benefit for obvious reasons. A blow because of the institutional nature of these theatres. They can become like little theatre factories. Get one show off of the assembly line and move quickly on to the next. This trickles down into all departments.

I wanted Grusha's baby in *The Caucasian Chalk Circle* to be created with purpose and imagination, you know? But understandably — if disappointingly — a prop department that is wildly underpaid and incredibly overworked can start to fall into the assembly line mentality. This sort of thing was *killing* to me — the kind of environment where those making the art have forgotten that they care. It would break my heart. Especially when I, myself, was also so fatigued.

The institutional theatre also suffers from the need to satisfy a subscriber base so that they'll want to resubscribe, which results in a lot of decisions being made for other than artistic reasons. I'm not saying that we aren't all aware that we are in a *business*, but the pendulum can swing too far. So much of this is about economics, of course. It's like Hollywood. As movies get more and more expensive, the pressure to make big ol' hits every time becomes incredible, and so there are focus groups and such, which put pressure on directors to change their work to appeal to a larger audience. And this is true for theatre. There is pressure to have everything be *spectacular*. Unfortunately, this is in such opposition to what art is. And it's in opposition to life, for heaven's sake! We are meant to fail. Failure teaches us. Failure helps us grow. The greatest playwrights have written flops. Some of them have written many flops. That's how they became great. Risk and failure are vital to art.

Disenchantment with the Lifestyle

On a more personal level, I came to understand the enormous physical, emotional, and psychological cost of doing eight shows a week. It is, on the most basic of levels, a very demanding life. And I saw that what it could afford me financially was never going to provide me the kinds of things I needed to sustain myself in that life — things I would need to do to take care of myself but that cost money. As my work was getting better, the roles I was being offered tended to become more and more complex and challenging, and that made those things all the more important. Stage acting alone was never going to allow me the time or money to travel, for instance — to really get away and refresh and open myself to new things that could feed my acting. And what about children; how would I do that?! I didn't really see a future that was feasible.

Strangely, or not so strangely actually, I had begun to feel worse as I was more valued as an actor. I remember being asked to come to some benefit event at The Goodman Theatre in Chicago. There were these very wealthy women dressed to the nines who were coming up to speak to me about how much my work had meant to them. As I listened to them, I began to realize that all I was doing was trying to hide my worn-out shoes. And I remember thinking, "Thank you, yes, and thank you for being at this benefit and supporting the arts, blah, blah, blah, but it's hard for me to hear how much you supposedly *value* me when I don't even have a decent pair of shoes and I'm not sure how I'm going to pay my rent!" I was just plain tired. And I'd lost my sense of humor indeed.

Going to Hollywood

So I went to L.A. in large part because I thought, "I just can't keep doing theatre anymore right now. I need a break!" And I wanted to see what L.A. was about.

I did fine in terms of the business — did my television guest spots, did a pilot, did all that kind of stuff. But I don't think it's a very good town to go into without a pretty clear picture of what you want out of it. I hesitate to say even that much because there are no "shoulds" whatsoever in this business. It's that fickle and wacky. But for me, at least, not having a particular agenda wasn't good. Going from working so much, as I did in Chicago, to sitting around most of the time — I didn't do well with that personally. And professionally, most of the material that I was reading for was … well, a far cry from Chekhov and Brecht, you know? And money, alone, wasn't enough of a motivator. So I couldn't get myself that inspired. On top of that, I didn't say no often enough to the questionable stuff; I sat across from too many twenty-year-olds who seemed to be running the industry (which was very scary); I waited way too long outside of offices for auditions — things that started to eat away at my self-respect. All of this adversely impacted my acting, not surprisingly.

The New York/L.A. Split

Here in New York, I can audition for film and television, but there is so much more of it in L.A. And many of the auditions in New York for L.A.-based projects are done on tape, which doesn't work as well for me. It's when I get in the room with the director that I have the best shot of getting a role, and being in that room also gives me information about the director and whether I want the part if I'm offered it.

My agent, Susan Smith, has been profoundly patient with me and my life and my career and letting me do what I needed to do; any other agent would have let me go ten times over because of my career choices. And even she has said at times, "The bottom line is that I can do more for you here in L.A." She would have liked me to move there, but in the end she's made peace with the fact that this works for me. I am extremely lucky to have someone as sensitive as she is to an actor's needs. This is very rare apparently — and unfortunately.

Building a Career by Doing Both

I have realized, though, that even with my career trajectory in New York the-atre, it's still unlikely that I would be asked to do a leading role in a large venue. If I continue to build my career primarily on the stage, it's almost impossible that I would get to do that; producers of any major production would feel that they have to cast someone famous — and fame means televi-sion or film. Or someone semi-famous and British. We have this odd idolatry of the Brits here.

There are exceptions to this, of course, but most producers are just too ner-vous to risk. They want the known, which is unfortunate for us all, I think, because fame does not necessarily correspond with one's ability to take on a great role on stage. So even if a name pulls people into the theatre, if they are underwhelmed by what they see, will they return?

And celebrity often creates a lopsidedness in a show. All the press, all the buzz, becomes about that. The play becomes a distant second to the famous person. I think it's lovely when I open up the *New York Times* and see an article about someone who has a great, interesting body of work or about somebody new who's doing something different or challenging. But I've also thrown my *New York Times* across the room when I see a full page on some second-rate film or TV actor who is getting this huge amount of coverage and legitimization for having decided to do a play. And it's often seen as such a daring and noble thing that they made such a decision! That kind of stuff can drive a person crazy.

Differences

Film acting requires something so different that sometimes even actors who have done a lot of stage work early in their careers can lose their stage sensibilities. It's such a different aesthetic, and the requirements of the two mediums are worlds apart. I hear actors say that it's all the same thing, basically. Not so, in my experience.

Film is inherently intimate, but there is always the distance of its not being a live thing. And there are certainly obstacles to overcome: the camera or mike is in your face blocking your view of your scene partner, or whatever. In working on film, though, it is more of the real world in some ways. There's a very intimate energy that's created because the camera is right on top of you and it can force you to mine an everyday truthfulness that's impossible to share from the stage. Seasoned film actors have their own technical specialties, but on a much smaller scale than in theatre; with the drop of an eye, you can tell a story on film. I love the challenges of the visual nature of film. It's very sexy to have that camera catching every blink and the mike catching every breath. And the possibilities of performance because of that are intoxicating.

The theatre is seemingly more distant as a medium, but I think it's very intimate. There is a body of people out there, sometimes inches away. Audiences are very different from performance to performance, and the story needs to be told specifically for them at that particular performance. In film, much of the telling of the story is done in an editing room. In the theatre, the story is sent out there and the audience responds, and all of that energy is manipulated as the story unfolds.

And the nature of how one sends it out there is a world in itself. I had the opportunity to play The Homebody in Tony Kushner's *Homebody/Kabul* in three different theatres. And the specifics of each space had a large impact on the choices I made in the performance of it. Just in the vocal work, there were big differences. The Mark Taper Forum is a semi-thrust setting with a lot of carpet, which absorbed sound. The Harvey theatre at BAM is a nine-hundred-seat space with a balcony and hard surfaces, which made it almost too acoustically alive. These considerations are almost nonexistent in the work I've done on film.

I am also such a text-bound actor. That was a difficult aspect of my transition into film and television. For me, the words have always been all. Everything is to be found in them. The thrust of the story is all about that. My job is the mining of the text, and that's what I get great joy out of. If I'm working on great, complex text, I learn every semicolon, comma, and period, because a great writer means different things with each one. And all those words, put together in their very specific way, become something that you can actually ride on. That's what it feels like at times.

But film, ultimately, is a visual medium. The text is not as central. It used to be really shocking to me to see people just making it up, saying whatever they felt like. I'd think, "But the writer! The writer!" Yet that's expected, you know; you're expected to be able to improvise in certain situations. Some films are entirely improvised. I'm much better at it now, though I still think it's not my strong suit. So many years of working with extraordinary *words*.

The Lessons of The Homebody

I'm curious to see what's around the bend. I've had such a remarkable experience working on *Homebody/Kabul*. I did a fifty-five-minute piece at the beginning of the play. And it was a mind-boggling piece of text. People often refer to it as a monologue, but it wasn't a monologue; it was a scene. It's just that my scene partner was the whole audience.

It is very, very rare in this country — or most countries — to have had the chance to work on something like that over a period of five, long, wonderful years. And to have had the opportunity to share something so intimately with a large group of people was very moving to me. It's basically ruined me. In a culture that is increasingly about how to make a faster, bigger, louder buck, I learned, more deeply than ever, the unquestionable richness and beauty that come with time. And also how meaningful it can be to have that kind of connection between actor and audience. I mean, I've always known that, but now it's in my *bones*. So, while I continue to work in film and television, it's just hard to imagine experiences of the magnitude of the ones I've had in the theatre. They've been so potent.

Homebody/Kabul is an important play. It's hard for me to work on something that isn't — although, sometimes what's important to convey isn't a big, huge thing. But that play is about the big stuff. And I've been so lucky to work on a lot of those. Mike Nichols said of Tony Kushner and his work on *Homebody/Kabul* that he was writing about what it means to be a good citizen. Which is what I want to be.

I'll continue to seek out the stuff that challenges. And I also know that it's vital for me to have variety in my work. I've happily built up a career that includes all mediums, including voice-over work, which I enjoy. I am a much better person and actor now that I exercise more of my muscles, as it were. And, though I love using the muscles that are seasoned by my work on stage, I do love the ones that get exercised in front of a camera. The question is, can I find the equivalent of the depth of movement there?

18

Robert Brustein

*American director and critic Robert Brustein served as dean of the Yale School of
Drama and founded both the Yale Repertory Theatre and the American
Repertory Theatre (A.R.T.), where he continues to work as a creative consultant.
He has served as drama critic at* The New Republic *and published numerous
books about the theatre, including* The Theatre of Revolt, Who Needs Theatre,
and Dumbocracy in America. *This interview was conducted in the spring of
2000.*

Cinematic Theatre

Since the advent of the screen as a dominant force in everybody's life — the
computer screen, the television screen, the movie screen — it's unassailable
that audience attention has waned. As a result, a lot of writers are now writing
in a cinematic rather than theatrical style. It shows in the episodic way the settings change, in jumps in time: no one observes the unities anymore. That's
the style of our time: these quick, brief scenes; it's like the frames of a film.
And since patience is much more limited than it used to be, you find shows
getting shorter: an hour to an hour and a half is about fairly average for your
typical new play. David Mamet started this trend, but others are following it.
Or, rather, plays are either very long or very short. Either you are going for a
four-and-a-half-hour Robert Wilson spectacle or you are going for an hour
and fifteen minutes of a new play. And I think that has to do with the fact that
the audience likes to switch channels; it's not used to having to look at something consistently. It doesn't like to have to work.

   Take *The Lion King* and *The Green Bird*, both directed by Julie Taymor. Neither
has stars. Both have music. The only difference is that *The Green Bird* is an
Italian eighteenth-century classic; *The Lion King* is a kitschy movie. The
kitschy movie is a success and will run for 50 years because it has all these
spectacular stage effects. Now spectacular stage effects can also be found in
The Green Bird, but people won't buy the story — it demands too much of
them. The spectacular effects are much easier to deal with in *The Lion King*
because you don't have to concentrate on anything else. So one's a great
success and the other is a failure.

High and Low

Great theatre draws on popular forms. Shakespeare, preeminently, would mix his lofty tragic scenes with a burlesque turn, like the porter scene in *Macbeth*. Charlie Chaplin is another example of a great maker of drama who can be lowbrow and highbrow at the same time. Even T. S. Eliot's *Sweeney Agonistes* is based on vaudeville and minstrel shows. So there's a healthy demotic side to the best theatre. And it may be that there has been a division in the twentieth century — a kind of split off of the healthy vaudeville tradition from the other traditions. I see it in the way the *New York Times* and *Boston Globe* critics review comedy and farce; they are repelled by anything that they would consider low. Farce, burlesque, vaudeville, and slapstick are low to them; whereas I see them as the source of a very healthy, exuberant energy for the theatre. I regret the loss of the old burlesque, the stripper shows, which had some of the greatest comedy I have ever seen. Bert Lahr came out of that world, and Milton Berle and Sid Caesar and so forth — all the people who provided the comic energy of Broadway in its heyday.

Exclusivity

There's no denying that theatre is exclusive. It's not exclusive of a certain *kind* of person, but it's exclusive. A theatre can't accommodate more than, what, somewhere between one hundred and one thousand seats a night, and that means that the thousand-and-first person can't get in. Whereas you can always go to a movie; if you can't get in one night, you can go the next, or if you can't get into one theatre showing it, you can go to the next theatre showing it, or you can get it on DVD or video. That doesn't mean that theatre is an elitist form, although it may become that way if things keep going as they are. But to maintain its "theatreness," it has to limit the size of its audience. A theatre audience has to be small enough to be a community.

Community

The audience once had a kind of hunger for going out and sitting next to other people. But we've gotten to the point where you don't have to leave the house at all in order to do your banking or communicate or entertain yourself. As a result, people feel safer in their own homes than they do on the streets. But at the same time, they miss the streets. And you have to go out in the street — you have to be with other people — to go to the theatre.

It's interesting to me that even in the movie house, people prefer the isolation of home TV. You really don't want anyone else there with you; you want to be alone with your fantasies. When someone comes and sits next to you, you move to another part of the theatre. Whereas, if you are sitting with empty seats on either side of you at a play, you feel as though there is something wrong; you want to be next to someone, even someone you don't know; you want to share with that person the laughter or the grief, whatever you are responding to on the stage. So theatre remains a very communal experience, while the screen in all its forms remains a solitary one. Theatre is essential to our lives for that reason — because it socializes us, it makes us part of a community, in a way that the other media don't. It's the difference between being a participant and a voyeur.

Theatre As an Event, Theatre As a Place

I think theatre has always been as important as a social event as it is an artistic event. People get themselves ready to go to the theatre; they invest a whole day in going to the theatre, not to mention a whole week's salary. You get dressed, you take your car or a train, you go out to dinner … it's a ritual.

It's also a schlep. One of the reasons commercial theatre is waning at the moment is because the schlep is costing so much money. You pay for the parking, you pay for the babysitter, the restaurant, the theatre tickets, and you could be buying one hundred shares of IBM. And if you don't like the show, there's no return on your money, so people want to be absolutely certain that the show is going to be the greatest thing they've ever seen. That's why critics have to use hyperbole to get audiences into the theatre, and it also explains all those weird standing ovations; it can be the most awful claptrap, but people are rising to applaud their own expenditures. You spent that much money; you'd better think it's great.

Now, there's another kind of theatre, which is a more relaxed, "drop in and don't bother to buy your tickets ahead of time" kind of theatre — the regional theatre, the Off-Broadway theatre, the Off-Off-Broadway theatre. The audiences for that kind of theatre don't just go to see the current hit at the Ethel Barrymore or the Brooks Atkinson. Instead, they go to a particular *place*, they go to *their* repertory theatre, because they are familiar with the actors or they are familiar with the style of the theatre and they recognize each other; they are part of a community. They are often invited to join in symposia or preshow talks, which have both an intellectual component and a social component. So the audience becomes part of a community. Audiences trust those theatres in a way that they don't trust the commercial theatre.

Those are the kind of audiences we have at A.R.T. We have seven to ten thousand people every year who come to the theatre as a place, not as an event. But it still depends on the critics to some extent, which breaks my heart, because the single ticket buyers still depend on reviews, and the reviewers are not trustworthy; they are never trustworthy.

Economics and Geography

Economics is something we can't fight. We are completely bamboozled by Hollywood economics. We — and when I say "we," I mean the theatre, and especially the nonprofit theatre — simply can't compete for an actor who is desired by Hollywood. The reason for the health of the British theatre is that both the film and the theatre industry are in London, whereas ours are separated by the three thousand miles that lie between the two coasts. You simply can't commute; either you're sitting around the pool in Hollywood or you're freezing to death in New York. And when you're sitting around the pool, you are immersed in a powerful and corrupting culture. Every actor worth his salt knows that is happening to him or her and regrets and bemoans it, but the material rewards are just too appealing.

Naturalism

I find that most theatres that are really worth their salt are doing just the opposite of what the movies are doing. Good theatre recognizes that, in order to survive, it can't pretend to be the movies. What theatre used to pride itself on — in the age of naturalism, the age of the Actors Studio, and the age of naturalistic playwrights — was that the audience could lose themselves in a particular play, would actually think it was real. They'd put real hot and cold running water on the stage and toilets would flush and there would be a sense of reality about it, and you'd be peeking at this reality through an imaginary fourth wall.

But now — and this is one of the great advantages of the current period in the theatre — we don't have to do that anymore because that's what the movies do. The movies can establish a documentary reality, bring us into the actual places. They are not filmed on sound stages; the actors are actually in the Colorado desert. And that frees the theatre to go back to being what it began as, which is a place of imagination, a place of fantasy, a place where someone says, "This is the Forest of Arden," and we're in the Forest of Arden just because the actors said so — you don't need real trees growing in order to prove it.

And the other aspect of this is that actors no longer have to pretend that the audience isn't there, and the audience doesn't have to pretend that the actors are unaware of their presence. The actors can talk to the audience as they used to do in the presentational days of Shakespeare and the Greeks — they can talk to the audience, deal with the audience, walk to the audience, bring the audience on stage, and make them another character in the play, a very necessary character in the play; whereas the audience simply can't be a character in the movies.

It used to be the great handicap of the stage that it pretended to be real when everyone knows, for instance, that if you talk in a normal tone of voice, the audience won't hear you. So how do you make your acting seem natural when you have to project in this unnatural way? There's a lovely moment in *Six Characters in Search of an Author* when Mme. Pace comes out and she's addressed by The Stepdaughter and they whisper to each other, and The Manager is saying, "You can't do this in the theatre, we have to hear you, for Christ's sake." And they say, "What we are saying is much too intimate to be shouted in a loud voice." That kind of conflict is intrinsic to theatre, and the best response is to say, "Look, actors talk louder than other people in order to be heard, and there it is. You must suspend your disbelief and you must also acknowledge your disbelief."

What passes for naturalism is always a style. When Marlon Brando broke upon our consciousness with that seemingly naturalistic Stanley Kowalski in *A Streetcar Named Desire*, people thought that they had never seen such reality on the stage. It was the perfect example of "the illusion of the first time." But we have the advantage of having that performance preserved on film, and when you watch it now, especially in the light of all the people who have imitated Brando since that performance, you realize that it was a style; it wasn't reality, it was a style.

You can find actors in Hollywood who are considered naturalistic, but who are really quite theatrical: Robert DeNiro, for example, Dustin Hoffman, Al Pacino. I do think, however, that, on the whole, movie acting is not acting; it's behavior. You behave in front of the camera and the camera does the work for you. You don't have to act in the movies, and the best movie actors are the ones who recognize that, like Spencer Tracy. Spencer Tracy just played himself in front of the camera; he was always his own, very identifiable persona. Humphrey Bogart, Clark Gable, Garbo, all the great movie stars were simply behaving in front of a camera. In that medium, the camera and the director do the work. Very good actors, really first-rate actors, sometimes have a hard time adjusting to film acting for that reason.

Risky and Ephemeral

I think probably the element of danger or risk or change or accident is crucial to the theatrical experience — the fact that you know anything can happen on stage. The actor can fall down dead, a prop can fail to appear, the door knob will come off in your hand — those things keep an element of risk in the air. That element is what they are trying to recapture now with live television; after all these years, they are once again willing to risk the possibility of someone blowing their lines or making an error of some kind because they know that a sense of immediacy is crucial to the dramatic experience. Without it, you've got something canned.

I've often thought what a shame it was that the theatrical event was so ephemeral, that it was here today and gone tomorrow and you have no record of it whatsoever — even those videotapes are not really a record of a live performance. But then, watching movies that I liked very much twenty years ago, I actually give thanks for the ephemeral nature of the theatre, because you see an old movie again and you think, "What the hell did I see in that movie? Why did I think that was a great performance?" Now it looks very tinny and old fashioned; whereas preserved in memory it was something terrific. The fact that people don't need memories anymore, the fact that tape and film and digital cameras have substituted for memory — that is unfortunate.

19
Paul Scofield

One of England's most revered actors and a long-time member of the Royal Shakespeare Company, Paul Scofield created the roles of Sir Thomas More in Robert Bolt's A Man for All Seasons *(for which he won both a Tony and an Oscar) and Salieri in Peter Schaeffer's* Amadeus, *and played* King Lear *in Peter Brook's celebrated stage and film versions of Shakespeare's play. His other film work includes Mark Van Doren in* Robert Redford's Quiz Show, *for which he received an Oscar nomination, and the 2002 film version of Arthur Miller's* The Crucible, *directed by Nicholas Hytner. What follows is not an interview transcript, but rather text from a letter Mr. Scofield wrote in lieu of the interview that we were unable to schedule.*

Fame

Social acceptance for me is not the issue; nor should it be for any kind of artist, functioning as we do outside and beyond the boundaries of what is deemed to be society. The approbation of audiences is another matter; those who visit theatre and cinemas — their appreciation is of the utmost importance because their interest is in our work (or not, as the case may be) rather than in our "images." My feeling, also, is that, in the States, there is much respect for theatre actors and actresses; but, of course, it is a respect shared by far smaller numbers than those who only wish to see movies. And they are two very separate extensions of drama and comedy, with only the adhesive of the actor and the writer to bind them together. As for me, I love theatre as being my life, but excursions from that life into work in movies is also a vital experience and a refreshment.

Money

As for the *competing* opportunities that film creates for theatre artists: Are there not competing opportunities in all aspects of human endeavor? Perhaps this is only financial competition, which seems to be crucial for film stars and thus for all film actors. This, for theatre actors, as long as they are paid sufficiently to cover the welfare of their families and give them a reasonable living (and this is not always the case), is neither here nor there. The work itself is the motive and the stimulant. But perhaps this is of no interest to publicists, and gradually the actor becomes more interested in selling than in acting. I hope not.

Acting in Film and Theatre

Can one do both well? There is an aspect of filmmaking which is irrefutable and baffling: the fact that some actors and actresses have something in their faces and bodies, not always beauty, which is caught to perfection by the camera. This is pure fluke and bears no relation to their talent, but the performer who is truthfully excellent in theatre will be equally so for the cinema. Well, that's what I think.

Unfortunately, acting styles in movies and television have influenced acting in the theatre, because in movies the visual is more important than the aural. Films sell on what they look like; theatre makes its bid for success on what it says. The effect can then be that the actor inured to the camera has not the skill to communicate language. Are there generational differences in acting style? I don't think I can answer that question, but if there were no difference something would be very wrong.

The Audience

Theatre audiences are theatre audiences. They may have many differing reasons for their attendance, but the root cause is because theatre is living flesh and blood and breath. Nothing can displace the communication between actor and audience. An actor is *influenced* by an audience. Every performance varies with the response of an audience; sitting in a theater seat, you are part of a mutual experience. A screen is no substitute for that. Only those members of an audience who have rarely been to the theatre cannot listen; they are an evanescent minority.

Great Theatre

Great theatre is an unexpected happening, like a volcanic eruption; it can never be anticipated. It occurs as a source of amazement and shock, and of enlightenment. It cannot *always* be present, but it erupts from time to time. It cannot die and will always return.

20
Richard Eyre

Sir Richard Eyre was the artistic director of the National Theatre from 1988 to 1997. He has directed theatre, film, and television. He is also coauthor of the book Changing Stages, *a history of British theatre, and creator of the companion documentary series produced by the BBC. This interview was conducted in 2002 in New York, where Sir Richard was rehearsing* The Crucible, *starring Liam Neeson and Laura Linney, on Broadway. His film,* Iris, *starring Judi Dench and Kate Winslet, had just been released.*

Working with Actors

On the whole, it's hard to see what theatre and film have in common except that they use the same tools in one respect: they use actors. And I think it's not entirely a coincidence that recently, certainly in Britain, there have been several successful films made by stage directors — Sam Mendes, Stephen Daldry, Nicholas Hytner, myself. It's because we have a lot of experience working with actors and are completely unafraid of working with what is, after all, the primary medium of film. In the U.S., there's less of that crossover of theatre directors into film.

There is no set way to work with actors. I know some actors who benefit from huge amounts of research, deep immersion in a part, and who stay in character the whole time. And I know other equally good actors who are the opposite; for instance, Judi Dench, who does practically no research, and while you're setting up a shot, she will almost invariably be telling anecdotes or just chatting, and then just as you're about to turn over, she'll click into concentration and be utterly immersed in the role.

This is one of the ridiculous things about "the method": it could only be created by someone who knows very little about actors and doesn't understand them, because if you know anything about actors, you know that there are as many methods as there are actors, and by definition, every actor approaches a part in an idiosyncratic manner. To codify a single method is just crazy.

It actually doesn't matter how you achieve your effects, as long as at the moment the camera is turning, the thing is alive. So whether you've achieved that by several weeks of rehearsal or by no rehearsal, it doesn't matter. The reason that many film directors don't rehearse with actors is that they're afraid of them. They don't understand them.

For the director in the theatre, you're much more like a conductor, and if you have good musicians, good performers, then you are essentially conducting — you know, pulling that up there, pushing that down. Whereas directing in film, you are — with the screenwriter — co-inventing the whole event, because your choice of where you put the camera, where you move the actor, what's going on around, the way you cut the scene, the way you reveal something, is all in your control. And there's precious little the actor can do, even the most powerful and controlling actors.

I'm working at the moment with Liam Neeson, who is a wonderful screen actor. Now he wants to do theatre and is spending some six months doing *The Crucible* on Broadway. And you could say, if you chose to put it that way, that he's sacrificing several million dollars in order to act on stage. Why does he want to do it? Because he feels in control on stage in a way that he doesn't on film. He feels that in some way he's in charge of his performance. He can take responsibility for his performance and relate to the audience. He can be gratified by their response. He can work with other actors; he can take joy in the collective enterprise. Whereas in film, even at his level, he feels that he's effectively the creature of the director.

Actor Crossover

There is an element of demonstration in the theatre that is absolutely the enemy of real screen acting. You are playing something truthfully but having to project it to demonstrate it. Now that projection, if you filmed what was going on, would seem exaggerated on film.

Some actors — Ian Holm is one example — are great film actors and great stage actors. But there are a lot of very good theatre actors who don't really work on film because they're too mercurial. What you need in the theatre is to think very, very quickly. And that's exciting for an audience — to witness a brain working at the speed of light. In film, you have to slow down because an audience wants to see an emotion travel across a face like a cloud across the sun. That is why an actor like Gary Cooper was so incredibly alluring, because he had that ability of slowing everything down, so that you were with him all the way. That's half of film acting — somehow slowing it down.

I think almost the best screen actor ever was Cary Grant. He was a consummate actor, brilliant technician, and a wonderful impersonator. But I don't think he could have worked on stage. Or James Stewart, an equally great screen actor. Somehow their acting was highly, subtly calibrated for the screen. They didn't have the sort of bravura required to be a successful theatre actor.

The Marketplace

Just the business of getting a film made is incredibly complicated. There are only one or two people in the world who don't have problems setting up a film. And of course it's partly that everyone gets so greedy in films because some people make a fortune; some films take in an enormous amount of money. Most films, of course, don't. But that doesn't stop people [from] asking for preposterous amounts of money.

A lot of actors aren't actually prepared for the corollary of fame and great wealth, but you think you want it. Though it has to be said that at least as many as crave money and fame are simply very, very good actors who are very pleased that they get paid a lot of money.

An idealist would say that it's easier to preserve sanctity — a primacy of values, art over commerce — in the theatre than it is in film because film is such a grotesquely expensive medium. It's quite hard to make a film for less money than I made *Iris*, which is six million dollars. But six million dollars is an enormous amount of money. And people talk about these tiny independent films made for three million dollars, but you get two plays on Broadway for three million dollars. And then, with a film, they have to market it. And this three million-dollar film, with no stars, is actually more difficult to market than a one hundred-million-dollar film with Tom Cruise and Julia Roberts, so you then have to spend at least three million dollars marketing it. As a result, almost anything in film is going to be millions of dollars. And I don't blame anybody for putting commercial pressures on the people spending that money. I mean, who says that anyone should have artistic freedom at that sort of cost? So it's a weird beast, I think, film.

The compulsion on most movies is in some way to uplift, even though life doesn't have a happy ending. The pressure is very much on to provide redemption, spiritual uplift, to lie about the world. You would be hard pushed to make *King Lear* or — if there could be such a thing — its "equivalent." Even with "modest" films of ten million dollars, it's a huge amount of money, and investors want some assurance that they're going to be able to get it back. There will be pressure to appease popular taste, and that will mean that you're not going to tell the truth about suffering.

Of course, in the eighteenth century, they were rewriting the end of *King Lear*, which would indicate that this is not a new thing. But genius transcends all rules. We get a Shakespeare once in five hundred years. Right now, there's no Bergman, no genius whose force of vision can actually transform the commercial rules. Is it possible to imagine a Stephen Spielberg with the soul and sensibility of Bergman? I think not, because there's something about the commercial viability and pliability of a Spielberg that is completely inimical to the Bergman sensibility.

When people have had total artistic freedom in film, it was when costs were much lower and there were patrons around. Bergman's films, or Fellini's, mostly didn't make money at the time; they barely covered their costs. But those filmmakers had people who were patrons, and the costs involved were comparatively low. And they weren't paying movie stars. It's hard to think of people working now whose artistic integrity is wholly protected.

We've created a sort of apartheid between the serious and the popular. That's the point that I try to make in *Changing Stages*: for all that seeing O'Neill on Broadway in the '20s was a shock, they were actually putting his plays on, on Broadway, every one of them. And his plays are so wacky, some of them, they're insane. And yet the stuff produced by this incredible, willful, dogged imagination was on Broadway; that's just where shows got done.

To have that now, you would need much more education, primary level, about art. And you would also need to cut seat prices. The theatre and cinema never get to be in equal competition until their prices are moderately related. If I can go and see a movie for ten dollars, why do I want to go see a play that costs eighty dollars?

The Audience

The audience in film isn't being asked to complete the circle. The film isn't going to be changed by the audience. The only thing that will change the film is the projector breaking down. Whereas in the theatre, the audience helps create. I can think of a moment in a Robert Lepage play, *Dragon Trilogy,* an immensely moving moment. There's a mother with a daughter who is mentally retarded and who is taken by a nun into a home. There were only two actors in the scene playing the three characters, and in the course of the scene the child turned into the nun and took away the child's suitcase. And it was immensely moving. It perfectly, poetically told the story and at the same time embodied the action: the very painful institutionalization of the child. You simply couldn't render that on film — there is no way — because in the act of that happening, at every stage of it, the audience is involved imaginatively in making all the connections. And in order for those connections to take place, the audience has to be there, has to be a partner, a coconspirator, to that fiction. And in film they aren't by definition — they aren't there.

Of course, theatre is terribly vulnerable for all the reasons that it's effective. Something goes wrong, the audience withdraws their consent, and the whole thing collapses. Because it's so fragile, so frail, it has to be done well for the consent of the audience to happen. Well, a lot of the time it isn't. Most of the time. And so people get suspicious of it; they get disappointed because the only thing that makes the argument for theatre being an interesting medium at all is an interesting piece of theatre. And also, by definition, it can be enjoyed by only a small number of people at any one time. And it's expensive because it's so labor intensive; so it belongs to a socially privileged group of people. It's a vicious circle. People feel alienated from it, and so on and so on; whereas film is demotic, because it's mass produced and because it's disengaged, I think.

Theatre never has been demotic. You know, people say, "the ground-lings," as if they were working class, illiterate folk. Shakespeare's audience may have been less well off, yes. But here is a highly successful playwright who is doing plays that aren't being printed, that have to work at the moment the word is released from the mouth. There's no point in writing jokes if people can't understand them. And, on the whole, Shakespeare doesn't play down. Yeah, there are some bad jokes in *As You Like It*, but we all like bad jokes. And there are some fantastically sophisticated jokes. I think it's just nonsense to pretend that an illiterate working class audience would have understood them. Yes, people cared much more about language and word play because books were not widely available. But contemporary Shakespeare research would argue that it wasn't the London proletariat standing in the stalls. I don't think there has been any theatre, and certainly not Brecht's theatre, which has played to proletariat audiences. I think this is one of the great fictions.

Differences

From the point of view of a director, almost everything about the theatre is unhelpful when you're directing film because a film image is made up of the composition of the shot, the point of view that you've chosen, the movement of the camera, the lens in the camera, and the way that you're using sound. In the theatre, almost invariably, you're putting the focus on the person who is speaking, whereas in film, by no means: dialogue is sometimes incidental, sometimes it's a background, an accompaniment, or it just is there to resonate against the image that is on the screen.

And a theatre production grows organically day by day, as you gradually accrete layers of meanings and texture to the performances. The sum of those performances makes a production, makes the *mise en scène*. But in film you're creating in the moment. You record it on film. There it is; one tiny segment of the film.

Essentially, if you look at the characteristics of the media, theatre has at its center, irreducibly, a live human being and a live audience. And you can't actually change the scale of the human being; it's always there. And you can't change the nature of the human voice; you can amplify it, but essentially you're relying on those frail human things.

But I think the single most important thing about the theatre is that it's always poetic. Everything is a metaphor; everything stands for something because it's not real and you know it's not real. It all relies on an act of imaginative commitment from the audience to subscribe to the fiction that it is real. You have a lamppost and you say, "It's a street." You don't need walls; you don't need three-dimensional things in order to conjure up reality. So it is engaging the imagination in that sense. Whereas film is quite literal. You look at something on film and it just is there. It's very, very hard to make film not be literal — for it not to be a street.

Of course, film is not literal in all hands. Look at Bunuel's films. They're not surreal because they have spooky special effects or the Daliesque design; they're surreal because he puts the conjunction of two entirely improbable real events next door to each other. Like the scene in *The Discreet Charm of the Bourgeoisie*: they're having that dinner party, curtain down one side of the room, and the curtain rises and they're sitting on stage in a theatre. In that sense you could say the "literalness" of it is hugely to its advantage. It's been turned to poetic advantage. But usually film is just what you see, and the audience is being asked to believe in a literal sense that something is happening.

And yes, a film can take you to fifteenth-century Japan in a way that the theatre can't. But there's something so dogged about it. There you are in fifteenth-century Japan, but everything has to be reproduced; whereas in the theatre you can have one object and someone coming on in a costume, a quite minimal costume, and the imagination of the audience supplies the rest.

It's why I direct theatre. Just that is at the heart of the difference for me: that theatre is a poetic medium — the metaphor of theatre, of things standing for things, the idea of an expressive medium that has that poetic power. It's very, very attractive.

21
Anna Deavere Smith

Anna Deavere Smith is an actor, teacher, author, and playwright. She is perhaps best known for her one-woman plays about racial tensions: Fires in the Mirror *(Pulitzer Prize runner-up and Obie Award winner) and* Twilight: Los Angeles 1992 *(Tony Award nominee and Obie Award winner), which Ms. Smith created from interviews she conducted and which, in performance, required her to deliver her subjects' words in their own voices. Her other writing includes a third play,* House Arrest, *and the book,* Talk to Me: Travels in Media & Politics, *which documents its creation. Her television and film work includes roles on* The West Wing, Presidio Med, *Robert Benton's* The Human Stain, *and Jonathan Demme's* Philadelphia. *Ms. Smith is the recipient of a prestigious MacArthur "genius" fellowship. This interview was conducted in February of 2004.*

Acting in a Diverse World

When acting becomes too much like what goes on in my kitchen, then I think it's not interesting. Stanislavski gave us a lot of things, but I think some of them were misunderstood, and this is one of them. To make it too normal also means that a lot of people aren't going to want to come because that artist's idea of normal — you know, for a long time, it was white men's idea of normal — is not the idea of normal for a lot of people. Normal is so relative, which is what makes realism a very hard proposition in a diverse world.

If Brice Marden comes here to paint you, it's not going to look like you. Maybe he likes the color of your eyes in relation to the color of your shirt, and he's going to do something with that; maybe that's all it is. He's an abstract painter. And that's what our skills as actors are supposed to be about. We have to leap off of reality. I'm not a Jewish rabbi. I'm not Al Sharpton. What the audience is looking at, what they are really responding to, is that I *try* to be them. They are watching to see what's going to happen: Am I going to do it? Am I going to make it?

To me, the problem with the human genome diversity project is this wish that we would reduce our differences. I think now it should be a different question. Our differences are here; now, how do our differences inform the human experience as we understand it? It's not that we should strive to make the gaps any smaller. They are what they are. That's why I like the idea of trying to become another character. You cannot, it's impossible, but you find something else in trying. When I'm acting, I'm not Anna, and I'm not Thurgood Marshall or James Baldwin or a Jewish rabbi, or whomever I might be trying to portray. I'm not that, and I'm not this; I am, as Richard Schechner puts it, "not-not," which is a positive and a different thing. And so it is that we are not all Japanese, we're not all black, we're not all gay, we're not all straight; we are this assemblage of not-not. It is not a melting pot, it's all the not-nots; it's a different thing entirely, which I think is a lot more dynamic. Real assimilation doesn't really happen; it's not even an ideal.

Presence

There are people who are very, very charismatic on stage who are not charismatic on film, and vice versa. Some actors are very photogenic on film but just cannot deliver on stage. In either case, the job of the actor is to make the project special to the audience, whether by making it emotionally present or by causing desire in the audience. Did they create a present moment so that they bring this text into reality? I remember the first time I ever saw Greta Garbo on film, she felt very, very present. It's charisma.

On the stage, if there is any reason that you don't like the presence of an individual actor, just on a sensory level, you will have a hard time getting through that evening of theatre. It's different in film because your eye is going to move; maybe there is a chase scene, there's a setting, so you don't necessarily dwell on any one actor. But theatre is hard to watch if there are any problems, and so the pressure is really on an actor to be imminently watchable. You have to want to watch that person; that person has to command your attention.

Now on television, you have to be likeable; people have to want you in their living room. They are less forgiving in a way. Even someone like Katie Couric will tell you how distressing it is that she keeps getting mail from women about her hair; you know, "I don't like your hair." So, you have to be likeable on television; you have to be watchable in theatre.

I don't think you have to be as likeable on film. There are people who have written about this much better than I can. I'm just bringing together pieces of things people have said to me, but I think a movie star has to fulfill your deepest desires — desires you don't even know you have. They are taking you to a really deep wish.

Different Rewards

The thing about film acting is that it is not, "I'm designing the character"; the editor and the director are. I am making a contribution, but I'm not creating the character. I am trying to give something that becomes a character, but they ultimately create that character. It's a different way of working.

When I do my plays, it's the opposite — and especially because nobody knows the character like I do. The director doesn't; the director has rarely seen the people I interview, and even if they are famous, the director isn't there when I do the interview. The director is certainly not huddled away with me when I am bundled up in some small space involved in the terrifying process of trying to cram all these lines down my brain. So I'm learning the character; the director isn't.

By contrast a film director believes he knows that character. Of course, each film is different. Sometimes the director wants to engage with what I think and I want to engage with what he thinks. And sometimes it's somebody who's talking to the cameraman and that's where his collaboration is and I get one take and he says, "Got that," and we move on. So, I'm very humble about that. I understand what you are giving up when you walk in there. It is artistically satisfying in a different way. You have to step back and look at the whole piece. Unfortunately, the way films are made, actors are rarely a part of making that whole piece. But if you can step back and look at the whole piece, then you see what somebody thought of what you were doing and what it was going to end up being. So I do it for the collaboration, for sure. The way that film directors think, what the set is like, what the other actors are like, you know, all of it is very interesting.

Television is another matter. The thing that I've loved about television — serious television — is that every day I get to go and try again to make this character. I can look at my work and know that I can try again next week. I can look at past episodes and see this, that, and the other about the director or the lighting. I can go to the costumer and say, "Well, what do you think about my hair. Don't you think ... ?" These sound like silly things, but they are what the audience sees.

On stage, I don't think about any of that, you know; it's just me out there trying to have command of the language.

Creating a Hybrid

In some ways, film is more liberating than theatre. I've just seen two very interesting films that are doing something new: one is *Dogville*; and the other is a film that didn't get treated very kindly in the press, called *Strip Search*, by Tom Fontana and starring Glenn Close, for HBO. It just came out — sort of a post-9/11 world where people are questioned, stripped, and searched. And both of these films are very, very heavy on language. And *Dogville* is not only a lot of language, it's also all shot in a bare room. I saw it at Cannes and people hated it; they got pissed off that it was three hours long and that they had to sit there and there was no scenery.

But these are like a new form of theatre on film, and in some ways it's a more interesting form than theatre. Theatre is very hard to watch because we come from a world of film in which the director's imagination carries our eye to many, many places and we can look at many, many things and there's the close-up and all of that, whereas theatre has only one frame. I thought that *Dogville* was very successful not only because it was engaging, but because it really delivered a new thought. It suggests that language-based writing has more scope than just the theatre. I hope it is successful because it seems to me that we need some new hybrid we haven't seen yet.

Hot Speech

The use of language in America is just at an all-time low for so many reasons. I have been teaching since 1973, and in that time my students have gotten wealthier and more educated, but their voices have gotten smaller and flatter. And that's coupled with the loss of courage that happened when somebody came up with this term "political correctness." It's a very bad term that has killed a lot of civic conversations, a lot of questioning, a lot of passionate discourse. And one of the things I've been doing lately is going back and reviewing some of the older dialogues that were captured on tape, like Margaret Mead and James Baldwin, Lorraine Hansberry and Mike Wallace, for example. I want to listen to them because conversations like these absolutely collapsed in our country once people began accusing other people of being politically incorrect if they had questions about certain things. So we don't really talk to each other because we are afraid to be honest. I can't imagine what this has done to intimacy or what's happening in people's relationships, but I don't hear a lot of really wonderful conversations in my classroom.

At the same time, we have in younger kids the so-called spoken word movement. I've learned a lot from hip-hop. When I go to see it, I realize that I'd better not even dare get up onto the stage ever unless I am totally present and have a feeling of urgency about what is coming out of my mouth.

When I studied Shakespeare, we studied speech as action. It's the same thing. When I go to speak at a college or whatever, I've realized that I should not be there unless I am prepared to expect of myself that the words I say are going to make a difference. No word can just drop out of my mouth when I am on stage; each one has to be potent.

And that calls for a certain kind of preparation that I don't think most of my students have when they come to study with me. They don't come to class with the expectation that when they open their mouths, not only does it matter what they say, but they should want us to hear, they should want to make a difference. So that this coolness, this kind of laid-back thing, un-animates the potential of speech. It's definitely not cool to be passionate. I am trying to make it cool with people I interact with, you know. I am trying to make it, well, not cool; I would like it to be hotter. I would like it to be much hotter.

Authoring an Audience

Raisin in the Sun and *Caroline, or Change* are both on Broadway right now, and both of them offer a potential polemic for civic discourse and a way of thinking about the past that can help people who do social change to think about the future. But in general I think we could be more creative about how we use theatre for such dialogue. It's really not just the play itself; it's the event we create out of it and how we think about the audience in relationship to that event.

Film has a whole other way of thinking about marketing. A lot of times, film people will tell you that their marketing is better than the product. But in theatre we usually rely on reviews to create buzz. So the success of *Raisin in the Sun* in attracting a young and very diverse audience — that is a great success. The authors of that experience are as much the people who created that audience — the producer and the marketer — as the artists themselves, and they are very aggressive about how they get that audience.

Eric Schnall is marketing *Raisin in the Sun*. He wanted blacks. And not just blacks. He wanted a young audience. And he got it. We can say it's because of Sean Combs, but it's not just Sean Combs. Schnall has street teams and he does a lot of work on the subways. He is taking everything he can learn, not just from black theatre, but from *The Vagina Monologues* and *De La Guarda* and *Rent*. He understands how to get people into a theatre in a different way with a different expectation.

The gap between that and any other type of marketer is really broad. You have to set out to do it and you have to understand. He tells me he goes home exhausted on a Wednesday night, and at 10 o'clock he finds himself thinking, "I wonder what the audience is like?" and runs down to the theatre to see. This is a person who really wants to do this and has a different idea of the audience.

I really wanted those people for *Twilight in Los Angeles*. They did not come; we did not find them. You are asking people to come in a society where they have so many options of how to spend their time. And it's really hard to get the people to come out of their own cultural understanding. There's a story I tell about this.

I wrote *Twilight* about the Los Angeles riots. I named it after a gang member named Twilight Bey. He never came to see the play. He didn't live very far from the theatre either. A couple of years later, I was at the Million Man March in Washington. There was Twilight. So for years later I would say, "How come you came three thousand miles to see Farrakhan, but you can't come around the corner to see the play?" It was a joke. So, finally, I hooked up with him again when I made the film of *Twilight in Los Angeles*. I said, "Twilight, why didn't you come?" And he said, "Well, you know, I really wanted to be there for you. You know, like, I barely made it to my daughter's junior high graduation. I just don't have the time." So he thought that coming to the theatre was to be there for me, to support me, to congratulate me.

Part of this is about the psychology of the actor and the psychology of the playwright. The theatre revolves around that psychology. It's like the wonderful scenes in the very beginning of *The Seagull*. They're putting on the play, and the young playwright Treplieff is so distraught because his mother doesn't watch, she's not paying attention, and that's the worst thing that could happen: your own mother doesn't even watch. Because, you know, the basic psychology of an actor could be that nobody has been watching and so therefore they've got to have strangers watch it. Or you wish you had that mother who comes running backstage, looking like Jane Alexander when she was young, saying, "Oh, Sweeties, when you were up there, my heart was beating so fast and I could not look at anybody but you." And some actors had that experience. So, that's what we think about.

But that's not sophisticated enough for the world right now. We have to be thinking about the audience as something that has its own integrity and its own voice, and how do we anticipate that and how do we make a collaboration between that and what it is that we are trying to say. Audience development has to be about what it is that I as an artist am trying to say and to whom and for what reason, and it has to build an audience specifically around that.

So now here's *Raisin in the Sun* breaking box office records: they are number ten with a straight play. It doesn't happen. It's not even an August Wilson audience, where the producers strive for diversity and count on, for example, black churches, you know; it's a whole other thing. It's tapped in. I think the problem with the usual discussion about audience diversity — and why it was so much fun for me to talk to this guy, Eric Schnall — is that it is too much like temple or church, too much like, "This is what we should do. This is our higher selves, trying to be fair and equitable. You know, reaching out." But when it's really working, it's not like that at all; it's very edgy. And I am sure *Raisin in the Sun* will inspire more of that. I think that a concerted and imaginative effort has to be made to bring the people to the theatre with the expectation that they are coming not just to see a play, but to actualize it in their lives.

In *Gangs of New York*, there is this incredible theatre scene in the Chinese Theatre or somewhere like that. And the way the theatre was — with the yelling and the screaming and the boos and the laughing, the candles and the lights — it was an occasion. All these people pressed into one room, you know; it's what we would imagine Lincoln and Douglas would have for one of their debates. The whole thing was a scene, so it was okay if it was a silly play because it was really about the entire thing — the people, the audience screaming up at the stage, the music, the lights, the President coming in, and so on. When that sort of an event is gone, that's when we start getting into problems.

Nobody Is Listening

There is a crisis of education among black and brown peoples. It's outrageous; it just breaks my heart. I just worry so much. I am disappointed so much that civic discourse is at an all-time low. I am beginning to think that the power and wealth of America must not really depend on people being educated, and that's why we can see this outrageous lack of education, lack of language skills, lack of understanding about what it means to do a job and what service is, and most of all what it means to engage. We can come into a restaurant and the busboys just throw something down, the waitress barely speaks; we call to get a phone number, and we say, "The New York Public Library," and they say, "Can you spell that?" Nobody is listening.

I lost my voice for four weeks this year; it was a virus that hit my vocal cords. I had to be careful when I spoke. And it was very clear to me that I almost always had to repeat something. Almost never was I heard, even with the simplest things. Are the nightclubs too loud?

Creating a Listening Audience

But now let's talk about Sean Combs on Broadway in *Raisin in the Sun*. He's not an actor, and because everyone is watching him be Sean Combs, he's not Walter Lee Younger. But the effect is very suggestive because it opens up and animates the text in a way that would not happen with an actor who trained in the theatre who you would expect to deliver that role. It's more interesting in a way.

What is, in the end, quite moving and quite wonderful about Sean Combs's performance is that he is kind of standing over here and Walter Lee is over there and he is saying, "Look at Walter Lee." He's not saying, "Look at me"; he's saying, "Look at Walter Lee. Look at this whole thing." I don't know that Sean Combs would think this is a compliment, but to me it's a really generous thing. He's almost like the host of this event and, you know, he's throwing a great party.

And his presence brings with it an audience who would absolutely otherwise not be on Broadway at all, maybe not for the rest of their lives. And the fact that we are all there waiting for something to happen, and that there's this great anticipation — Is he going to make it or not? How well is he going to do?—has this ripple effect of creating a listening audience. It creates a listening audience that is hearing Lorraine Hansberry's text again in a brand-new way.

That kind of listening doesn't happen in film, not just because of the language, but because we're not present. There is a certain pleasure in the reality of the sound of the human voice. Like when a preacher takes the whole crowd to another place or when a great orator did that in the past. We don't really have much of that in our society anymore because politicians don't do it. They are not trained to do it; they are trained to be telegenic instead. So nobody is really speaking to the ear anymore. It's not Lincoln and Douglas anymore; politicians are not speaking to the heart, and they are not speaking to the ear.

You could say, then, that the theatre should completely occupy that territory and make sure that it always, always delivers that because it is a rare thing now. But I don't know that many theatre artists really think about that part of their storytelling. Musicals do it; they know that people want to hear the song. But I don't know how much we think about it in terms of straight plays.

In putting together my plays, you know, I am listening over and over and over again to what somebody said, to try to find a landscape of language that will take the audience to someplace else that they might not have gone. And in large part I am banking on the fact that they haven't been listening in their daily lives, so they haven't heard this before. There's just so much to listen to that is hard.

You know, one of the best compliments I ever got was from Woodie King, whom I have admired for so many years and who ran the New Federal Theatre here and who produced, among other things, *For Colored Girls…* . And Woodie said of me at a conference once that when I come on a stage, basically what I am saying is, "You know everybody. I just want you to hear this. Somebody said this to me, and I can't believe they said it, and I want you to hear it, too." It's like the old days of bringing your friends over to hear records. The artist, Lorna Simpson, talks about how, as a girl, all of her friends would come over in the summertime to listen to Richard Pryor records. I think a community can be created around that listening.

So I guess this is a very long sloppy way of saying that the theatre is a place for the listening audience, and there is something about that that is very important. We should assume that the audience is coming to hear something, and we should think very carefully about what it is we want them to hear.

22
Robert Falls

Robert Falls is the artistic director of Chicago's Goodman Theater — a post he has held since 1986. A number of notable Goodman productions directed by Falls have transferred to New York, including Tennessee Williams's Night of the Iguana, *starring Cherry Jones and Bill Peterson; Arthur Miller's* Death of a Salesman, *starring Brian Dennehy; Eugene O'Neill's* Moon for the Misbegotten, *starring Cherry Jones and Gabriel Byrne; and* Long Day's Journey Into Night *starring Brian Dennehy, and — in the Tony Award-winning New York remounting — Vanessa Redgrave. Falls also directed* Aida *on Broadway. This interview was conducted in the fall of 2002.*

Parallel Universes

The theatre is always being threatened by every new medium that comes along, be it radio, silent movies, or talkies, and yet it always seems to prevail and flourish. I don't really view other media as competition, but as parallel universes. Theatre just happens to share any number of artists and craftspeople with those parallel universes, who move back and forth or leave one forever or for a certain period of time.

The thing that is most commented upon is that the medium of film has attracted writers away from theatre. People who formerly might have written exclusively for the theatre have found themselves working exclusively for film. Why, I'm not quite sure, because the writer has a lot more power and influence in the theatre. But in any case, you find very few people who have completely left the profession. Great novelists — Faulkner, Hemingway, Fitzgerald — all had their try at writing Hollywood screenplays for money, and I think it's the same with theatre artists.

Pay/Prestige/Power

Among theatre, film, and television, theatre still has the highest prestige. Of course, it's the lowest in terms of the overall pay scale. And actually it's now television, even more than film, that's at the top of the pay scale. We all know Tom Cruise makes $25 million a movie, and there are a few other people who make that kind of money, but, for the most part, the real money to be made — for writers in particular and to some extent for actors — is actually in television, which is seen by many more people than film, and by many, many more people than theatre, but yet has the least cachet of the three forms.

For writers, television is similar to the theatre in that the writer can have power by becoming the writer-producer. So you see somebody like Aaron Sorkin, who created *The West Wing*. Aaron Sorkin's is a case of a playwright who wrote a play, *A Few Good Men*, and then immediately went into the film world with the film version of *A Few Good Men*, and ultimately found himself as an enormously powerful, influential person in television.

Among artists, especially, the theatre still holds a sort of mystique. But clearly, film is the principal medium of the culture. Everybody wants to be a film director. You can ask an eight-year-old what he wants to be when he grows up and he'll say, "A film director." You ask anybody out of college. Nobody wants to write the great American novel anymore, but they always say, "I want to be a film director." So that has a mythology all its own.

Influence of Film on Writing

As a result of the influence of film and television, there is absolutely no doubt that plays have gotten shorter, sharper. It's rare that you find a playwright writing in long sustained verse, the way Tennessee Williams or Eugene O'Neill could sustain a narrative through dialogue for fifty continuous minutes. Increasingly, you get shorter and shorter scenes that correspond with the short scenes of film and television, and the younger the writer, the more they tend to be influenced by that sort of "short verse" writing. But I don't know that it matters. It simply goes with the territory.

It's often been said that the audiences' attention spans have gotten shorter as a result of television, but I don't know if that's true. The origins of our theatre were in an incredibly aural society. People talk about Shakespeare's time — the puns, the complexity of the language that an Elizabethan audience could absorb very quickly because the ears were everything. Even reading was completely secondary to hearing. But an Elizabethan would have no idea what to do with the bombardment of visual images that we're accustomed to processing: I think their brains would go on overload if they saw the quick cutting and imagery that film and television use. So the culture has absorbed those quicker plays and those writers who are writing them in shorter verse. I don't think it's necessarily a good or bad thing; it's simply where we are.

There's a lot of moaning about, "Where are the great plays? Why aren't they writing plays like Shakespeare or Aeschylus or Eugene O'Neill?" I don't think that's fair. I think there are many, many great plays for our generation. I think actually we're living in a golden era of playwriting right now. I was thinking about this subject last night, and I was able, off the top of my head, to make a list of 135 writers whom I find to be really interesting writers — American writers; I didn't even go into the English writers. And these writers write far more interestingly than virtually anything we see in film or on television, which has to be done by narrative or visual images or melodrama to some extent. Writers ranging from Tony Kushner to Regina Taylor to August Wilson to Richard Greenberg to David Mamet to John Guare to Marie Irene Fornes, Spalding Gray ... I mean, I could go on and on and on with writers who are writing on all sorts of subjects and moving people and saying interesting things. They have an audience and it's an active audience, though it's not the same audience that Aaron Sorkin has when he writes an episode of *The West Wing.*

I've heard it said that working in Hollywood can compromise a playwright's voice or distract him, but I don't think that's true. That's an arrogant statement that implies writers are like children — that they can be seduced by some bad guy in a car with a lollipop, that they get in and are driven away. What underlies that is some sort of romantic notion of the playwright as a pure artist. I think that's bullshit. Artists are grown-ups, and I think that they're more than capable of moving back and forth among the different media. David Mamet has done it. Steve Tesich did it. Writers do it all the time. Not all of them can, of course. Marie Irene Fornes is one of America's great writers, but I don't think she has any desire to write for Hollywood and I don't think she could adjust her voice to do that if she wanted to. But others can. And some writers come back from Hollywood as more interesting writers because they've broadened their ability and their freedom.

The Acting Drain

With actors, the talent drain *is* a real problem. That's a very tricky situation. Probably the broadest impact Hollywood has on the theatre profession is as an incredible draw for actors. And that's been going on for a long time. We were working on *Death of a Salesman* here at the Goodman. Arthur Miller talked about Lee J. Cobb giving this legendary performance as Willy Loman — one of the great performances of all time — and then electing, really shockingly early on (I don't think he made it through a year playing it on Broadway), to leave to do, as Arthur Miller says, "some God-damned Western on the RKO lot" which offered more money. Now, again, that's a sort of human thing, you know; actors aren't children either and they're going to do what they need to do to support themselves and their families. But it does often make it difficult.

I wouldn't necessarily call it a talent drain, but there's no doubt that when one is casting a play, one often has to come to Hollywood or television for the best talent to do that play. And for the most part, agents would prefer to see their clients do television or film because it's going to be a higher salary for them, which then trickles down to the agent. There are cases where you put an offer to an actor and the actor never gets the offer from his agent; you're told the actor got it and turned it down, but the actor actually never got the offer. That's a very common story; it's not an urban myth. And it probably wouldn't have happened twenty-five years ago. But for every case where an agent tried to discourage stage work, I've had the other case where the actor wants to do a play and the agent is doing everything they can to figure out a way to make that happen.

Admittedly, I don't think most agents care about theatre. They are businesspeople; they're there to get their clients as much money as they can. Every once in a while you meet an agent who is working closely with an actor, thinking about the overall arc of the actor's career. But actors are very practical. And again, I don't get too upset about it. In fact, I'm always surprised when an actor who's in demand will do a play because I think, "Why shouldn't they make as much money as they can?" The fact is that the theatre has let down actors by not paying them for their talents. And they want to work on as big a playing field as they can, and, for most actors, that is television and film.

Most good actors can go back and forth. Of course, there are also many theatre actors who are deemed "too big" for film, and there are many film actors who are deemed "too small" for the stage. Movie acting depends upon a whole different energy that the camera picks up — a sort of magic that isn't always recognizable on the stage. And vice versa: you can have an extraordinary actor on stage who simply doesn't work on film — who seems too hammy or doesn't seem special on film. There's a sort of alchemy that's a mystery.

As an example, I don't know whether Robert DeNiro would be particularly interesting to watch on stage anymore. His specialty is an inner life, almost a black hole of energy. In film, you can achieve a sort of stillness that's almost a negative energy and that allows people to watch you intensely. I'm not sure that would be interesting on the stage. But there is a remarkably large group of actors who have no trouble moving back and forth between the two worlds — trained actors for whom it's simply a matter of modulating voice and expression. Somebody like Al Pacino, for example, is every bit as interesting when you see him on stage as he is on screen. He's a fantastic stage actor — daring, you know — just out there and theatrical and fantastic.

But you really can't be a star in this country without a film career. There's no such thing as a theatre star, really. There is a small category in New York of "Broadway stars" — people who will sell tickets to Broadway shows who are not film stars. Mostly they do musicals. But to be a star in straight theatre almost exclusively depends on film and television. Of course, being a star and being an artist have absolutely nothing to do with each other, and that has always been true.

The Audience

The cliché is, "Oh, you can't take young people to a play three hours long because their attention spans are too short." I've said that myself. And there's no doubt that young people have been far more exposed to quick cuts and edits and fast and loud. But my production of *Long Day's Journey Into Night* was four hours of O'Neill, and I saw it performed in front of sixteen- and seventeen-year-olds who sat absolutely silent and got totally and deeply into it. I think they found it a deeply rewarding and unusual experience to be called upon to focus and concentrate for that long. So there's a sort of handwringing that I'm not sure is really borne out. I mean, if something's bad, I don't want to sit through it and you don't want to sit through it. We can't just make blanket generalizations that kids or young people or an audience won't sit through something long because, if it's good — if it moves them, if they're touched by it — I think they will.

Church

We're always wringing our hands over the death of the theatre. And at the same time, *Time Magazine* yearly runs the story, "The Death of God." And there's a connection, because theatre is really close to religion in some ways. People go to church or synagogue or whatever their place of worship to experience something communal and spiritual. And theatre does that too, whether people come knowing that or not; they're met with something spiritual — actors telling a story, hearing language, being in the presence of a community of people watching. There's something there that is addictive.

Different Things

A play is a different thing from a movie or film. I go see all sorts of movies because I want to have the adrenaline rush of a roller coaster ride. I get bored very easily sitting in a movie that I think would be better as a play. People will say, "Oh, did you see this movie? It was so wonderful. You know, there were four characters in a room ... ." And I would be bored stiff by that, because that, to me, is a play. And as much as I love watching *The Sopranos* every week on television, I wouldn't want to see any of those stories in a theatre. Theatre wants more resonance. It has to be metaphorical; it wants to have a bigger idea behind it. Even if it's something simple like Chekhov. Chekhov is about small moments between people (and many playwrights are more Chekhovian than they are Brechtean or Shakespearean), but there can be something wonderful about seeing actors engaged in small moments that are divorced from the thrusting narrative that is generally required of television or movies.

Theatre can be as much about silence as it is about noise, whereas silence is an anathema to both television and film. You just cringe if you're sitting in silence — visual silence or aural silence — in front of television or film; whereas the theatre lives in its silence. Silence is a part of theatrical language, like the rests in music. A playwright has to have an ear. Again, it's like music. Every good writer writes a kind of music. Even if their plays are about inarticulate people — like Mamet's or Rebecca Gilman's, or Franz Xavier Kroetz's — there is still a certain music and poetry to the language.

But I'm not particularly drawn to theatre that feels like literature. I love literature, but if someone talks about "literary" theatre, that has a negative connotation for me. I get a little tired, for example, of literary theatre in the sense of debate or argument of the kind the British theatres are full of. I prefer theatre that touches things that are intensely human.

Theatre Is Alive

Theatre is so alive, as opposed to film. People say, "Oh, movies are what's real because the camera captures reality," but actually it's the theatre that's real because the actors are really there and it's dangerous, and it's closer to the circus or a basketball game because the actors can get hurt. There's something thrilling about the danger: the lead actor could have a heart attack or he could forget his lines, he could trip over a table, or a lighting instrument could fall and stop everything. And because any number of things can happen in the theatre, it's alive, and I think the audience senses that.

Film is packaged. It's moving in front of us in a preordained continuity, and that's comforting to us. And, to some extent, we expect a theatre performance to be like that; we expect that they're just going to do what they always do. But each performance in the theatre is unique, which is something that theatre artists are aware of and audiences generally aren't. You may think you're seeing the exact same thing that your neighbors down the street saw, but you're not. And when something goes wrong in the theatre, those are the most memorable nights to audiences — you know, when an audience member goes, "I was there the night that the sets stopped" or "I was there the night that the prop didn't work." Those shocking moments remind us that, no, everything we're watching is alive and happening and fluid in front of us.

I don't think audiences are aware of how much they impact a performance. Everyone in the theatre constantly refers to the audience. "How were they tonight?" And the actors will say, "They were good" or "They were bad." But when you go to the theatre, you don't think of yourself as "the audience." You may have a perfectly wonderful time and love what you just watched, and then you go backstage and the actors say, "Oh, you saw it tonight. It was a terrible audience," which means, "You were a terrible audience." You find yourself being given a blanket judgment by the theatre artists. But it is true: an audience takes on a collective personality night to night.

Cultural Prestige and Art

For better or for worse, theatre has become so minor. Theatre used to occupy a much more central place in the culture, but that was for a brief period of time — mostly in the '20s. And to some extent that's a blessing because you just don't worry about these things anymore. There is an audience for the theatre, people come to the theatre, and they get tremendous pleasure out of the theatre. It's never going to be the movies. It's never going to be the television. It can't because it just can't reach; it's closer to a "ma and pa family store" on the corner than a Jewel or an A&P.

But here's an interesting fact: far more people in this country go to live artistic events than go to live sporting events, though you would never know that from the way it is covered in the media. More people go to museums, plays, concerts, ballet, and opera than get in their car to go see a football game, basketball game, or baseball game. But pick up the newspaper and you see there are twenty-two pages devoted to sports and three pages devoted to the arts, two of which are about pop culture.

I just finished reading a book of essays by Dominic Dromgoole. It's stunning, also very controversial. He takes 150 playwrights, mostly British, and he writes about them completely candidly. I mean, how this guy continues to work I have no idea. Mostly he writes positive things; maybe ten of them he's highly negative about, including some of England's principal writers, like David Hare and Tom Stoppard and a few others. But it's really passionate; it's a great book.

Anyway, this guy was an artistic director with a small theatre company, The Bush, in London, and during the ten-year period from 1990 to 2000, he discovered a lot of very interesting young British playwrights. He writes passionately, in this earth-shattering prose, about these evenings of theatre they were putting on. He was right at the center of this. What he was doing was exciting and vital and innovative, but I was thinking about the fact that you couldn't have spread it much bigger without losing something.

He talks about that — about how there is a popular culture and there is art, and let's not pretend that these two are related. Let's not call Aaron Sorkin a great artist, because he's not. He's a fine, fine craftsman, but he's not an artist, you know. Marie Irene Fornes is an artist. August Wilson is an artist. There is such a thing as art, and we would like to have more people exposed to that than to popular culture, but it's extremely difficult to do now and I think it's always been extremely difficult to do. I always remind myself when I get really depressed about this that down the street from The Globe was the bear baiting, and many, many more people were watching the bear get tortured than were at Shakespeare's theatre.

Critics

In the theatre, the critic has huge power. The newspapers and audiences treat theatre reviews like *Consumer Reports*. It's like restaurants: if they're going to be spending thirty-five to a hundred dollars for their dinner or their play, they would like to know in advance if they're going to a good restaurant or they're seeing something worthwhile. It's a horrific sort of hurdle that every play has to get through. In a perfect world, the audiences would discover the play themselves.

Here's an example: One of the greatest experiences of my life was a play by John Guare called *Landscape of the Body* that premiered here in Chicago in 1977. I saw this play and it was a life-altering experience. I thought it was the best new play I had ever seen, just transcendent and moving and funny. It was just getting ready to go to New York, and I expected it to be the sensation of all time. Well, it was crucified by the New York critics and ran about three weeks and it just disappeared. And I was stunned. It was a production that had received a very positive response here in Chicago, but it was destroyed in that particular environment. I can't explain it.

Overall, arts journalism has gotten sleazier and sleazier and more dependent upon the pop culture and gossip and speculation. Or it has all to do with the critic and very little to do with what they're watching on the stage.

Even take someone like Kenneth Tynan. He was entertaining — a brilliant writer and a brilliant essayist — and there are moments when he'll take your breath away. What he did that was most extraordinary was to capture the experience of seeing a certain production. In that way, he's right up there with the very greatest critics writing in the English language. So to read him on *Long Day's Journey Into Night* in its original production is thrilling because he really captures something about that production. And he advocated for some of the most important plays of his time. But Tynan is also a good example of somebody who was just so completely fucked up and filled with self-loathing and complexities and power hunger that he couldn't be trusted. He was wrong as much of the time as he was right. He made huge mistakes and was quite corrupt as a critic: he had his favorites and he curried favor with them, and he knew he had influence and he liked to wield that influence. So overall, as a critic, he was as reprehensible as the rest of them.

And this is particularly a problem because we depend on critics more than we used to. There used to be more newspapers in Chicago. There used to be more newspapers in New York. Now there are so few voices. By contrast, film critics have no impact whatsoever. Absolutely none.

Creating an Event vs. Putting on a Play

One of the biggest problems I face as a producer is that every play has to be an event. You have to create an event to get peoples' attention, to get them into the seats, so you want to have a star actor or a star director or a play that's sexy in some way. It's not enough, it seems, just to do a play. We're very fortunate here in Chicago because there's a lot of theatrical activity. But even here, just to get attention one feels one has to do something spectacular, which is an enormous pressure on the institution and, God knows, on the artists.

I don't think I've ever had a situation where working with star actors has been detrimental, though. There are star actors who also are very good actors, and fortunately we're not under any pressure to fill the seats with the star who is wrong for the role. I don't think most people are. But trying to cast stars does bring lots of headaches logistically. I'm in the midst of it right now with our production of *Long Day's Journey Into Night*, which was originally intended to transfer immediately to Broadway. *Death of a Salesman* was such a success that the same Broadway producer went out and got the rights for *Long Day's Journey*, which was a big deal because it hasn't been on Broadway in fifteen or sixteen years.

But instantly I was in a dilemma. In Chicago, I did it with one star, Brian Dennehy, who also happens to be an actor I work with all the time, and two Chicago actors and a New York actress and I thought it was pretty terrific. But nobody wanted to see that version in New York. And that angered me, until I finally got it that New York is really about seeing four stars. Chicago isn't. Chicago is about doing the play. New York is about seeing four stars. Broadway is, for sure.

That's the wonderful thing about Chicago; people are just doing the plays. It's impossible in Chicago to become a star or a failure. You just do the play. If it works, if it's a hit, that's great, and maybe that furthers your career a little bit, but not that much. And if it's a bomb, it doesn't hurt that much either. In New York, a smash hit could be career-making, and a huge flop could be quite devastating.

Of course, as a result, Chicago is a way station for young actors. Young actors are ambitious and, if they're really talented, they want to have the largest sea to swim in. But look at Steppenwolf. The great news about Steppenwolf is some of the actors do come back. They created a system where, yes, they do go away, but they also come back, and I think that's the more noteworthy fact.

Doing Both

Hollywood pays a lot of lip service to the fact that theatre directors know how to direct actors, but ultimately they aren't going to give you money on the strength of that. There has been a rather disappointing history of theatre directors given the chance to direct who have made rather plodding, cloddy, nonvisual films. And that's no good, no matter how well acted they are. And I don't think that producers and money people in Hollywood actually give a shit whether something's well acted or not. It's much more important to them that it looks good, moves fast, and has enough style.

I'd very much like to do film. But I think that the American film industry is not particularly weighted towards using theatre directors as film directors — unless they're British. I actually can't think of that many American directors who move between film and theatre, you know, a few, but not many.

The British have a far easier time at it. Somebody like Sam Mendes or Stephen Daldry or Nick Hytner, you know — they're very, very talented, but I don't think they're necessarily any more talented than the best American stage directors. Hollywood recognizes a certain charisma in a British accent.

But, yeah, I would love the challenge of doing something different that's also similar. I think there are certain stories that are better told in film than on stage. Film is mostly visual, and it also requires a really strong story; the narrative is much bigger than language or metaphor or poetry. And it has to do with manipulating space, time, music, and rhythm in a different way. It's a different language, and I would love to explore that language because I admire it so much.

The attraction for me is not that film directors have more power. The notion of the film director as *auteur* is bullshit. In film, you need a really good script, you need really good actors, and you need a really good cameraman and editor and composer. The success of, say, Daldry or Mendes or Hytner is due to the fact that they're really good producers as well as directors; they know how to manipulate, seduce, and coerce all these people into doing really good work for them and then they have the ability to hold the movie in their head. The key to being a director in both film and theatre is marshalling all these other people's energies to do their best job. And there's nothing particularly "*auteur*" about that.

On the stage you do the same thing, but there are more variables in film. Really a director has more power in the theatre. You're never fully in charge in the movie world because you've got all these money people involved. But those are some more of the people you have to seduce, manipulate, and coerce; well, seduce anyway. And it's worth the effort because the reward is creating something that has a life that you can hold onto. The ephemeral quality of theatre is frustrating. It's extremely frustrating. Yes, it's satisfying and beautiful and moving to me to hear an audience member talk about their memory of a treasured performance — an experience of being in the theatre that has become a part of their being. But there's nothing left except what exists in memory. There's no other record of it, you know; it's air.

And the other big payoff of directing film is the same as for writers or actors: more people see your work, and there is in our culture a bigger splash surrounding that. Not necessarily deeper, not necessarily more spiritual, not necessarily more fulfilling, not necessarily more prestigious — but bigger. What's that line from Mel Brooks? … Yeah, "It's good to be king."

23
Mel Kenyon

Mel Kenyon is a playwright's agent with the London firm of Casarotto Ramsay & Associates, Ltd. Her clients include Howard Brenton, Caryl Churchill, Frank McGuinness, Timberlake Wertenbaker, Stephen Jeffreys, Phyllis Nagy, Mark Ravenhill, and the late Sarah Kane. This interview was conducted in the spring of 2002.

Intrinsic Worth

Mythologies grow up around certain people. They're box office success or they're box office death. It creates a sense that art and commerce are always diametrically opposed, that nothing has integral worth; it only ever has financial worth. I would love to live in another world, where things actually have intrinsic value. So when you pick up a play, whether it's by somebody very well known or by somebody who is not known at all, that piece of work has intrinsic value. If it's a good play, whoever may have written it, you'd think that a good actress would want to do it. And if a great writer wrote a bad play, you'd think people would have the guts to say so. But it all gets mixed up.

So actually all you're trying to do is to combat these various misconceptions or mythologies with your own brand of truth — to say, "Believe me, this is actually good. I know." You have to be slightly mad; you have to have that fervent belief. Also, you have to be proved right enough times for other people to vaguely believe you.

My contention, when I was very young and even more arrogant than I am now, was, quite simply, "Producers can't read." Which is not entirely true, of course, but there is an element of truth in it. I've got this stupid idea that when something is really, really good, people know. So all you want to do is put it out there and make sure as many people get to see it as possible. The trouble is that between that belief and putting it out there are producers, actors, and actors' agents; you have to jump through all these hoops, and the last ring of fire you have to jump through is the critical one.

Critics and Audience Reaction

You sit in an auditorium where people have been told something is good; they are bored shitless, but they think it is their fault. You can be sitting there hating something, and you know that everyone else in the auditorium feels the same way, and yet somehow the denial is so overwhelming that they respond to it in a particular way and you just think, "Did somebody *pay* these people?" They have to believe that they loved it. They paid for parking, they paid for dinner and went to the show, and it was a big deal. That's part of going to the theatre — it's not like going down the block to visit the movies.

Critics can't always tell the difference between a bad production of a good play and a good production of a bad play. They can be completely blinded by the celebrity of somebody involved, whether it's the director, the leading lady, the leading man — even the venues achieve their own glamour, or not. So one season, every production at a particular theatre — whether good, bad, or indifferent — is seen as having a golden glow, and three seasons later, the same people can do nothing right.

I suppose critics are only people and sometimes they get it very right and sometimes they get it terribly wrong. I've worked in theatre all my life. I don't know what it is like to be an ordinary punter and pick up a paper and read a review and think, "I'm going to spend thirty-five quid on this ticket." You have to listen to somebody.

The question that is very difficult to address is how taste evolves. How do one's individual tastes evolve and how does collective taste evolve? How is collective opinion formed? This is why the critics do have a responsibility. They create history. It is frequently false history, of course. If you really believe what the critics and the academics say, then the '80s produced no great theatre in Britain at all. But some great plays — written, incidentally, by women — came out of the '80s. I mean, *Our Country's Good, Top Girls* - - all these extraordinary plays.

Counseling Writers

I had a dinner party row recently. Somebody said, "You will sell out, your writers will sell out, you mark my words, it's only human nature." Rather vociferous response from me. But, in fact, you know the writer, you know their sensibility, their work, what they're psychologically built to do. Over time, you have long relationships with these people. You know what artistically they can and cannot embrace and what will and won't make them happy, and you weigh all that up against the commercial viability, the money-making prospect or whatever, and you may well tell a client not to take a lucrative job because the money offered is not worth the damage that will be done.

In general, I think, writing for television does not marry easily with writing for stage. There's something about the very smallness of it. And those writers who have migrated towards television and enjoyed it and stayed there, the young ones anyway, I'm unsure how they can come back and write a great stage play. Something changes. Their writing becomes slightly anemic; it doesn't feel full-blooded. Some dimension has gone.

But you can also risk destruction of the writer; literally, the destruction of the writer. I've made one mistake I'll never forgive myself for, where I allowed a writer of enormous promise to write a screenplay too early, and she has not come back. She has not written again. She was just 24, 25, and she had an extraordinary talent and the project seemed absolutely right for her, and she was working with some very sympathetic and nice people, but something broke her back writing for the screen and she's never written again.

Of course, some writers are much more robust than others, and capable. So you make that judgment, in your head; you weigh up everything. How strong is their desire to make money? How delicate is their artistic sensibility? How precious is their talent? And I don't mean valuable, I mean precious. How fully formed is that talent so that actually it can take the knocks and come back again, you know, resurrect itself even if they go through a bad experience. And different writers may be capable of different things at different stages in their careers.

I have a young writer. She wrote her first play, successful in a small way, and then it actually went to New York and has been successful in a bigger way, and now it's come back here. It first went on in this small theatre, got very nice reviews — young, female Alan Ayckbourn, blah, blah, blah — and television people quite rightly started ringing me up, rather unusually. So she took some of the meetings and she didn't take others. Eventually, she was offered a place on what was called The Carlton's Writers Course. It's an independent television company, and they had a writers' course and they'd select six writers every year and would take them through the hoops of writing for TV, and then they would end up with a script. And she left after four hours there, saying, "I can't do this. It's so alien to me. They look on it as a product, and I can't actually think about my writing like this. I can't do it."

If a writer does not truly, truly want to do something, you must never allow them to kid themselves into doing it for the money because the writing experience itself becomes so hard. Getting the words down on paper becomes so hard that, unless it's hundreds of thousands of pounds, the money is simply not worth the psychological trauma. One of my writers took a job because he desperately needed the money — not because he doesn't earn money, mind you, but because he spends it. He was offered this project that he didn't really want to do and for three months we said, "No," but they kept coming back and he finally said, "Yes." He has been through hell because actually he didn't fall in love with the idea that he was supposed to adapt for screen and so he's cranking something out and you can tell. I mean, if it ever gets made, it certainly won't be his best work. You can feel the strain in every line.

Playwrights Can Have Good Experiences in Film and Television

Now I'm going to sing the joys of TV for playwrights.

You can't write four stage plays in a year. It requires having really original ideas, having something to say. If you are going to write a good stage play, your writing is an extension of you, and writing a really good stage play can take a lot out of you.

Film and television writing uses different parts of your writing persona. It's an intellectual and a technical challenge, but it uses different muscles. So sometimes when a playwright is really worn out after writing a play, writing a screenplay or something for television can be … well, maybe not a rest, but a holiday of sorts.

There's a playwright of a certain age named Howard Brenton — a wonderful playwright who wrote some very big, robust, dangerous plays in the '70s and '80s. He's a man of an epic vision and very far, far left in sensibility. The *Spooks* series came up. I liked the production company very, very much; they are really bright people. And I said to them, "I know this is crazy, but Howard Brenton is a fabulous writer who is kind of being neglected right now. He loves conspiracy theories. Why not meet with Howard Brenton?" Something just seemed right. And now he's doing it, and he's overworked and excited and doing extraordinarily good work and, as a writer, he is full of confidence.

David Harrower is a very beautiful writer. When he was thinking of coming with me, his first question was, "Will you ever make me write for television?" And I said, "Absolutely not." And now, seven or eight years later, he's writing his first screenplay. I think it's been in his head for awhile that he'd like to do a film project, but somehow we've both known that it wasn't quite the right time. And then along comes this particular project with a writer/director who comes from Scottish theatre, as he does, and they get on and he has written a very, very lovely first draft of a screenplay. And the writing is quintessentially his, but you can see he's exercising a different writing muscle.

Of course, the writer's experience depends entirely on how he or she is treated. I wish more film producers would understand that you are not going to get great work out of writers if you undermine them the whole time. They forget to say, "A lot of this is great. Let's just look at X, Y, and Zed." Instead, it's, "Oh, but we always go to seven drafts." It's an odd mentality, and I think it is about power, but nobody really will acknowledge that. Partly it's the notion that, because so much money is riding on it, you have to do ten drafts to justify spending the money.

Film people tell me all the time, "Mel, you don't understand, sweetheart. Film is a collaborative medium." Which means, "I can do whatever I want with your writing." And, "Oh by the way, you know, the writer isn't allowed on the set," says the director. Collaborative, my ass. Film people say that they collaborate, then they impose their will on others. In the theatre, the writer is still — to an extent, at least — allowed to be the writer. You write your play, it is done. That rules out all the middlemen and wrests creative control from those who don't actually have a right to it.

But with these two — touch wood — very positive examples of Brenton and Harrower, film can be seen as truly collaborative and the writers suddenly don't mind because everyone is on the same side, aiming for the same goal. The writer is feeling supported, understood, their intentions are understood, the script has been read properly, and suddenly they're there, willing to do rewrites, willing to go to meetings; suddenly they are not defensive creatures. But if you keep undermining somebody who is actually good at their job, eventually they are just going to go away, give up, or deliver bad work.

Theatre as Stepping Stone

This notion has grown up that, as a young playwright, you can train yourself in the theatre, get spotted, and then become a screenwriter; the theatre is just your nursery. Even some agents think that way: having a play on at the National is not regarded as quite the same thing as having a film made by Miramax. And, of course, it is true that if you have a notorious play on at Royal Court and your name is in all the newspapers, then people in the film industry are going to accept you as a writer, capital "W," far more easily.

This exploitation of the theatre and disregard for it as a real art form make me see red. I think it is more difficult to write a really good stage play — three-dimensional, metaphysical, metaphorical, visceral, philosophical — than anything else in the entire world. Great plays are few and far between. But also I think playwrights are born, not made. I really believe that you either quintessentially understand space and dramatic action or you don't. You can't teach it; you can only hone what's there. So the notion that somehow you grow up into screenwriting I find faintly ludicrous and insulting.

Bad Television/Good Television

Recently there was a television series: six parts, high profile, fantastic cast — just chock-a-block full of the best of British theatre, including Michael Maloney, Helen McCrory, Antony Sher; the list went on and on. But it was unbelievably badly written; everything was signaled wildly, underlined — "thematic concerns," "exposition." It was like ticking a box. There was one exchange where Michael Maloney gets into the car with his wife, and she says, "Oh darling, I didn't want to wait much longer. I almost had to go off and get the wine on my own," and he says, "Why are we getting wine?" And she says, "Because we're having dinner with my parents." And he looks glum, and she says something like, "Is that a problem?" And he says, "Well until I stop being a Jew and your father stops being a bigot, it's always going to be a problem." And I'm sitting there going, "Oh, my God, this is awful!" and "What are these fabulous actors doing in there?" Da, da, da. Critical response to it: fantastic! They think it is complicated, difficult, blah, blah, blah. And I think, "Is this the best we've got to offer, really?"

Now something like *The Sopranos*, that *is* fabulous writing: complicated, dark, sometimes even shocking. There is almost a signature on that, a voice of some kind. Tonally, it is almost unique. How they continue to manufacture that week after week, I don't know. They got it right and they managed to keep getting it right.

Television Audiences

Kids write, if they're not very good playwrights, very boring plays. One scene follows another, the scenes are short, they're episodic. And maybe those kids have sat and watched television, but to me they're just not very good plays. If you're going to write a play that just goes chmp, chmp, chmp, with little scenes set on an estate, that's not terribly exciting. Great playwrights, whether or not they've watched television, won't do that because it's not theatre.

However, what I think has happened is that those plays have become more acceptable as plays. So, particularly in the early '90s in the U.K., we had this supposed renaissance and a lot of young men writing a lot of plays which are really rather linear and literal, and all the critics going, "Oh wow, this is extraordinary! Look at all these brilliant plays!" Somehow that became an acceptable form of playwriting: very simple, linear narrative told in a very simple, straightforward sort of way, when there was nothing really to watch, no metaphor was achieved, there was no inherent image structure.

There was a lot of debate at that time, especially amongst the women who care passionately about theatre, asking why this is happening. And it was Phyllis Nagy who came up with a theory which I think is very valid. She said that the way television had infiltrated the theatre was not so much in writers' copying television, but that through television we've become used to receiving information in a very literal form of journalese. Television tells us what is happening. The news literally tells us what is happening in the world. And drama on television also tells you what is happening. You rarely see something unfold; you are more often told: "Oh, I feel awful today." We've literalized communication.

At the same time, you look at something like a car advert, which is so irrational. How is anyone supposed to understand why the car is going through a burning hoop exactly? You are fed with vibrant, violent, but ultimately meaningless images — a brushfire or a woman in a white dress in the pouring rain with a soundtrack — but there is no real connection at all to the content of the message.

So when you go back in the theatre, which is a place for metaphysics and metaphor, people have forgotten how to watch. They don't understand an image structure. What would *The Cherry Orchard* be like without the cherry orchard, the sound of the axe, the twang of the violin string? There's an inherent image structure, a substructure of the play. But people don't know how to read images anymore in that way because we're not asked to.

The full meaning of theatre is somewhere between your brain and imagination and that of the playwright; the two of you join in some kind of thesis, antithesis, and then synthesis. The play has an inherent meaning, but it also has the meaning you brought to it because it asked you a question. There are plays that ask rhetorical questions, which are the ones I don't like; they are kind of sealed and they just tell you, "This is my message." And then there are open-ended plays, which invite you to join in a debate. But people are so used to being told what to think now that I think sometimes really good plays just become too difficult.

The other way that television may influence people over time is the modern-day public hangings: Jerry Springer, Oprah's show. There seems to be this incredible thirst for melodrama. But you mustn't mistake the melodramatic for the dramatic. Melodrama is inherently bogus. There's a good guy; there's a bad guy. It's very, very simple. It goes right back to those simplistic Victorian dramas. It's almost atavistic, I think. I don't know whether melodrama appeals because in day-to-day life people are so bored that they hunger after something that is ludicrously overblown, something that takes them away from the mundane. I don't know.

Sentimentality

I get cross with myself when films are woefully sentimental and I find myself crying anyway. Show me a sports movie where the underdog wins and I'm in floods of tears. I can't control my response to that even though I know I am being manipulated horribly. But if that were on stage, I would probably walk out. I remember that Bill Nicholson play, *Shadowlands,* about C. S. Lewis. I got so angry watching the play, I thought, "Don't do this to me. Don't manipulate me like this!" I was sitting with my stepmother and she was crying and I said, "Oh, don't be so stupid." And I went to see the film and I cried. Why? Maybe one allows oneself that luxury when the whole relationship is so false. It's very odd.

Spectacle and Transcendence

Often when we see a movie with car chases and buildings being blown up and special effects, what we're relishing is the sheer extravagance of this commercial enterprise. Victorian theatres did the same thing: trains were going across the stage; they were creating this extraordinary spectacle. But possibly because film has taken over the role of satisfying our human desire for something spectacular, the theatre has become, for me anyway, something else. It's a place for debate, it's a place for philosophical thought, it's a place for beautiful language that is so rarely cherished now — and I don't mean lyrical, overripe, horrid language, but a place where you can listen to the rhythm of language, to a great actor speaking great lines. Where else are you going to find that? Something transcendental can happen in that space, and when it does happen, it is so extraordinary that you go back time and time again, waiting for that moment when your breath is taken away.

24
Tony Kushner

American playwright Tony Kushner is the author of the Pulitzer Prize-winning play, Angels in America, *and of the screenplay for the award-winning television version directed by Mike Nichols. Kushner's other stage works include* The Dybbuk, Homebody/Kabul, *and, with composer Jeanine Tesori,* Caroline, or Change. *What follows is compiled from two separate interviews: one conducted in December of 2003, shortly before the HBO broadcast of* Angels in America; *the other conducted in January of 2004, the day after* Angels *won six Golden Globe awards.*

Why Film Angels in America?

I'm not sure that I wanted to make *Angels* into a film. Now that it has all gone so well, of course, I'm incredibly happy that it happened. But by the time I was first approached about doing it with Mike Nichols, I had long since given up on it ever happening. I felt, "Well, it's just not to be," and, given how unlikely it seemed to me that it would work, I felt fine about that. I had spent eight years of my life writing and getting it on Broadway, getting the second part on Broadway, the national tour, and seeing it all over the world; it was my entire life in the '90s. It was really hard to think it up the first time, and I really didn't want to rethink it. I thought, "Okay, well someone else could take these basic characters and basic situation and then come up with an entirely new way of telling it. But after all of this work to tell it well for the stage, why would I in any way want to be the one to do that?"

Writing Screenplays

Film and theatre are completely different art forms that have very little to do with one another. Likewise, the business of writing a play and the business of writing a screenplay have almost nothing to do with one another.

My experience writing the screenplay for *Angels in America* was not typical because we stayed so close to the play. Every time I went away from it, Mike pulled me back: "You do it better in the play." And Mike has also been very theatrical in his direction of the filmed version. He kept the doublings, for instance; it was actually the first thing he said to me: "I want the actors to double as they do in the play." That is one of the reasons I wanted to work with him on this. But generally the forms are very different. It's completely not the case that film is in any way a replacement for or an improvement on theatre, or even anything basically akin to theatre.

I'm writing my third screenplay now. The first one I tried to write was a complete disaster. It was an adaptation of a children's book that I really love, *The Pushcart Wars* by Jan Merrill. Jonathan Demme hired me to do it, although it was my idea originally. I completely blew it. I couldn't make myself do it, to start with; and when I finally forced myself to try to do it, I wasted a year and a half on it and wrote this gigantic terrible mess. It was heartbreaking. Whereas I feel so totally at home writing for the stage; I am so completely in control in my head of the different elements involved.

But now that I have done the *Angels* film, the one thing that has really made it better, I think — although the screenplay that I am working on now is still difficult for me to write in a way that I don't know that a play necessarily would be — is that *Angels* at least played out on a set and I got to see what filmmaking actually is. That makes it a little less alien.

One thing that makes me insane about the form, though, is that you are writing a kind of sketch. In working on this new screenplay, I have to force myself to forget (and maybe this is what all screenwriters do) that what I am writing is going to be remade when it is shot and edited by a director.

Distance and Size

One of the differences between stage speech and film speech is the posture of intimacy. In doing *Angels* with Mike, I realized that one of the reasons you need big, heightened language in theatre is so that the thing you are looking at in the middle distance feels closer. The people are small bodies moving around on the stage, and that distance creates objectivity and a cooling of emotion, so the language has to rise to certain levels of passion, excitement, and electricity, even in just the music of it, to compensate for that.

Whereas, in film, you are not only in the action between two people who are having a fight in the bedroom, you frequently *are* one of the people having the fight, because the camera becomes the eyes of one of the two people fighting. So it's more than intimate, it's like demonic possession. And the language has to tone down as a result.

In filming *Angels*, Mike made the language work, but he uses a lot of tricks. For instance, he doesn't show people's mouths moving very much. You frequently watch the person listening rather than the person talking. Otherwise it would be too intense and almost ludicrous. It is equivalent to stage make-up, which looks weird up close, sort of shocking, because it is deliberately calculated to compensate for the cooling effect of distance.

Whereas, with the scale of film, you can show Gwyneth Paltrow's face the size of a building and you can show in incredible detail a gigantic battle scene like in *Lord of the Rings* or the whole Alpine mountain range or the planet

Earth, you know. Images in film can be so astoundingly beautiful and compelling and detailed and vast. I just saw the *Battle of Algiers*. You've never seen anything like it in your entire life; it's astounding. Of course, you can't always talk about film now as one thing. Cleopatra's face on a giant screen has a certain degree of overwhelming power; some of these actors are astonishingly beautiful and that kind of beauty has its own power that the silver screen honors. But that face becomes something else when you see it on a portable DVD player. There are many different things that we mean when we say film.

Television, of course, is much, much smaller. And audience expectations are smaller, too. Audiences are used to plays on television, in that sitcoms are staged, silly comedies. The dramas bring in a more cinematic feel for the most part, but even *Law & Order* could be done in a room; you don't need to do it in New York, as they wander around on what seems to be the same street week after week. It's all so stylized; it's the same formula, and what it always comes down to is the inescapable staple of all TV drama, which is the courtroom. And courtroom drama is a medium of talking heads, and the courtroom makes a theatre.

That's why I felt strongly that *Angels* should be shot for television, that people would find it much more familiar on television. It needed to be six hours, and it's more appropriate for a medium of talking heads. People love it on television and I love to see how people are watching it: hour by hour, all at once in one sitting, fifteen minutes here, twenty minutes there, two hours there. It's amazing; it's like they are reading a book.

The worst thing we could have done with *Angels* would have been to make it into a spectacle. We did bring tons of stuff over to Hadrian's Villa to shoot the heaven scene — billions of extras and angel wings and desks, and they were going to shoot this huge Hollywood extravaganza — but in the end you just didn't want any of it. All that you wanted was those actors.

I've said this a lot, but one of the things that Mike did in the film with *Angels* was to make the special effects always announce themselves as not real in rather creative and lovely ways. That's part of the theatricality of it because the generator of that kind of effect has always been the theatre itself.

The Psychosis of Digital Effects

As we get more and more into the age of incredible digital manipulation, certain anxieties I think are inevitable. We see in *The Lord of the Rings* this astonishing thing they have done with the Gollum character, which is clearly the prototype of something on the way that will become standard and virtually impossible to detect. There is so much manipulation that goes on already. And a certain percentage of the people will succumb to that without any anxiety because they are not really smart enough, or are too beset by other problems, to care. But some percentage is going to find that degree of successful illusion nervous-making, even if they enjoy it. I mean, it is in a sense psychotic, because you literally cannot tell the difference between illusion and reality at all.

Changes in the Audience

You can really depress yourself by asking whether or not some kind of permanent change in the human psyche and the structure of human intelligence is being caused by electronic media and artificial intelligence. If I were a parent, I would certainly be very leery of letting my children watch a lot of television early on. I think that television is probably a very odd medium for very young brains to absorb in enormous doses. But, you know, the onslaught is omnidirectional and universal and fairly irresistible, so I don't know what point there is in being wide-eyed about it and saying, "Oh, the world is so awful" and "Oh, it's all over and it was so much better fifty years ago," which in some ways it was and in some ways it wasn't, and when has that ever not been the case?

There are other trends that are less scary but very interesting: for instance, the fact that twenty- or thirty-somethings apparently don't buy theatre subscriptions, they buy single tickets. They don't get the idea that you should support a theatre as opposed to buying a product that you want. You want this play so you buy the ticket to go see it. Why would you shovel out all that money and commit yourself to a whole season with a theatre when you don't really know what the hell they are going to be doing and it could be bad stuff and, in fact, there will be bad stuff? Why would you do that? That's a huge generational shift, and, for the economics of theatre, it's somewhat alarming.

I think that is something that one could argue against and possibly even make an impact on. I mean, go tell the kids at Dalton and Trinity and the other places that are producing future fetishists with disposable income that the reason you buy a season subscription is to make an investment in the possibility of good theatre; you are buying that theatre's future so it has more money to play with and knows how to plan. Explain that if you are stuck on single ticket sales, you are going to get safer, less exciting programming. Out of every nine plays you see, you are going to hate six of them and two of the three that you love are going to be the same two that everybody loves, and then there's going to be this third play that you love that half the audience walks out on but that changes something important inside of you. That's what you are investing in. We need to talk to people about things like that, I think.

Anti-Fetishistic

Everything that has to do with the creation of consumers has to do with the creation of fetishists, and everything that has to do with the creation of fetishists is problematic in the theatre. The theatre is anti-fetishistic because it doesn't ever finish, it's never complete, it doesn't present you with a product that you can pocket. And so, the more people come to develop a sort of deep cathexis with their Lexus and their toaster and their flat-screen TV, the more complicated it is going to be to get them to develop a real relationship with real human beings — or with real human beings pretending to be fake human beings on stage. And I don't know what the answer is; I really honestly have no idea.

In the machine age, film can be a product. Did you know there's a film company called "The Good Machine"? Take my little PDA that you can watch movies on. This is an amazing device — it is a work of art in the age of mechanical reproduction. But it makes film into a product. This is one of the things that is always more appealing about film. You can go to it whenever you want and it doesn't cost all that much, of course, and now you can carry it around in your back pocket. So it is a commodity, it is a fetish object, it does not change, it is not organic, it will never be different one day to the next.

Here in the beginning of the twenty-first century, our relationship to the inorganic is so refined that we've eroticized it. Marx was completely right: we've totally fetishized things. And a movie is a thing — very human thing, but a thing. An argument could be made that film was invented precisely to help us become erotically attached to the inorganic, like the Lexus that you have to buy or your life won't be full; you can work at a shitty job, but as soon as you get in that Lexus and drive down the Pacific Coast Highway, suddenly you're a human being again. Of course, you can also say that theatre was invented by the Greeks to help create the kind of consciousness that would finally separate us from the world itself into a completely man-made, artificial world. But film was made possible by machines, the development of machinery, and it may be the machine's way of seducing us into responding to it as if it were alive so that we lose the distinction.

The Danger of Theatre

Film is safer. It's easier to go to. Not just because it's cheaper and because you don't have to plan ahead of time, but because you know it's going to be the same every day. You change, of course. So you may go see *The Lord of the Rings* twenty years from now and think, "Yeech." Or maybe you'll think, "This is much better than I remember." But it is the same thing and nothing that you do will fuck it up; if you get tired or you feel sick or you are bored or you are not in a good mood, you can walk out and not hurt anybody's feelings. And that's enormously appealing.

Film will also never embarrass you in a way that bad theatre will. You're not going to be humiliated by proxy, watching an actor in a terrible play or a bad actor on stage being humiliated, suffering through their embarrassment. You don't have to feel guilty afterwards for hating an actor in a part or hating everybody in a play or hating everybody in the theatre because they have gone to this terrible play, and then go home and feel bad because you've been sitting there loathing these other people. Film is all on plastic and they are gone. It's over, finished, and they are off doing their other things. They have aged, they have died, and whatever. You are not accountable to them or to yourself; you are excused from being a human being in your relationship to film, at least to the extent that you can't hurt it.

Whereas theatre won't allow you to escape the erotic and the human and the carnal in the same way, and consequently it's much harder work to sit through a play. Even rude, disgusting people who get up and stomp out of a play know the power of that stomping; they are engaging in the danger of the moment.

The danger of theatre is something you learn the first time you are doing a play with an actor who is elderly and they forget their lines — they "go up," as we say. It's very different when it happens with a young person; the audience seems to think that they have had a fuck-up and will get back on their feet. But the minute you see an older person go up, you know you are dealing with hardening of the arteries and the play is over at that point. It's terrifying as nothing else is. It's fascinating. In rehearsals with actors beginning to lose their memory, the whole theatre — as bad as people can be — will rally around them to protect themselves from what they are seeing. Because, of course, an actor not able to remember lines anymore is frightening; it's like everybody's mortality is staring them in the face. And yet that's also part of what makes it fragile and human and great.

Theatre Is Ephemeral

One of my favorite theatre artists is Elizabeth Lecompte, and one of the things I admire about her so enormously is that she doesn't allow the performance to become a finished object at all — I mean, it changes literally every single night. When Declan Donnellan directed *Angels* and *Homebody/Kabul*, he threw this tremendous responsibility onto the actors because — if they were good enough and if they wanted to — he gave them the freedom to reinvent the event every night. So what I saw one night isn't going to happen the next night, and then, of course, it goes away and is gone forever.

Jeanine Tesori and I were just talking about a director we both have worked with and admire who is famous — or notorious — for spending a long time setting up his production shots; you have to give up some of your precious final rehearsal time to somebody taking stills of the show for the press. There was a guy who did the same thing with Charles Laughton's company when they were doing *Bluebeard* — he took these gorgeous, terrifying images. Of course it's fake, but it's this desperate, heartbreaking gesture to trap on film this thing that is gone. Charles Laughton is dead. If you didn't see him, you didn't see him. You see him in pictures and films, but if you didn't see him on stage, you didn't see him.

There is a new book about the actress Duse that is a beautiful attempt to figure out what it was about her that made her so astonishing. And while you get a sense of it, it's also wonderful how much the book is vexed by the question of what she would look like to us now. And there's just a sense of loss.

The Degradation of Language

The degradation of language, especially in the political arena, is not a new story. The doubleness of political speech goes way back: that happened with Hitler, and it is something that Schiller certainly writes plays about. And you listen to these reality shows and it is immensely depressing because the rules of the language have completely slipped out of our grasp as a country; we don't know how to speak English anymore. And then, on the other hand, people mint astonishing new ways of expressing themselves that are so grotesque and comic and hideous and yet kind of fascinating.

My first theatre professor could tell, even though I was just starting out, that I was interested in writing a lot of language into my plays. He used to tell me that, in his pessimistic opinion, audiences hear only about 40 percent of what is said on stage. Percentages sound scientific, but of course, it's all hooey. I mean, it depends on where you are and whom you are talking to and what kind of words you are saying, how resistant an audience is to hearing them, how well you are delivering them, and how beautiful they are. But certainly an audience does not hear everything that is said, and people in the same audience will miss different things, and so on.

On the other hand, the hardest thing I ever wrote in terms of density of language is the Homebody's monologue. And I got more good press about that than I think anything I have ever written, including *Angels in America*. People love the monologue, and I think part of it is just the joy of this outrageous language. We still do Shakespeare over and over and over again and it doesn't get easier. It gets harder.

Owning the Language

There is a thing called table work in the first week of rehearsals that is almost always a waste of time. It's frequently about the anxiety and terror of getting started, which has everything to do with the fact that we don't have enough time to do these shows. You start a six-week rehearsal period — which is already outrageously luxurious by today's standards — and you are already months behind because you should have a minimum of three or four months with a play. So you can't bear to get up on your feet because the minute you do, rehearsal is over and it is time to do the previews and open and it's horrifying. So we throw away a week as if to say to ourselves, "We have time to throw away," when of course you don't. That week is frequently spent talking about what they ate for breakfast in Moscow in 1903 and what they would have had on the road to Sebastopol.

All that is nothing to do with what's really at hand, which is the language that you are going to have to get up on your feet and make believe is something that's coming into your head — something you own with the same intimacy as your own spontaneous utterances. But you don't own it; you have to fake it. So what I see Mark Wing-Davey do when he's directing Craig Lucas's play, *Small Tragedy* — and what other directors do who are really good at it — is just stop and stop and stop, asking, "Why is that a semicolon? You don't ultimately have to do it as a semicolon; you can do it as a period or you can ignore it completely. But what is the difference between a semicolon and ignoring it completely, and a semicolon and a period, or a period and a question mark?

I mean, why would the writer have done that there; what's the meaning of that?" And that kind of Talmudic investigation of the words, being smart about it and responsible, is at least one way that actors move into owning the language.

When people are just talking, their mind is processing and producing these words, which is reflected in pitching their voice in various ways and inflecting and curving and shading the voice. One of the reasons the British do Shakespeare better is because there is simply more musical fluctuation in British speech; American speech is a cramped and flatter terrain. But even when Americans talk, every word is pitched to a tone and it fluctuates and varies wildly and there is a fantastical variety and subtlety of expression.

But when you recite somebody else's words, a lot of that goes away. And there are some actors who have a certain kind of brilliance of presence on stage — they are there, they are exciting to watch because they seem very human — but they are uninterested in this somewhat artificial process of delivering speech both as though it is spontaneous utterance and also with the same kind of calculation that is involved in preparing an aria. Not many people know how to do it. These are the skills of actors like Stephen Spinella or Linda Emond — both of whom I love to work with. Part of it is just the technical training of the muscles of the mouth and the training of the mind to speak with a tremendous degree of specificity. These are certain technical skills that a conservatory-trained theatre actor should have, which is why I hate undergraduate drama programs. They don't train people this way because they really aren't old enough to be bothered, and it's also not an easy thing to teach and to be good at it.

Film and Stage Actors

What's sad to me is the number of really terrific young actors in film who simply don't develop the technical chops that a great stage actor needs. Stephen Spinella is a great stage actor. What Stephen can do — standing on a stage in a giant auditorium and seeming to whisper yet being heard in the back row — that's a trick; but it's a trick you have to learn.

You've got really amazing young actors, but they graduate from undergraduate drama programs and are sucked right into the Hollywood machine. And it really takes three years to train a stage actor; it can't be done as an undergraduate. I don't think you can do it when you are eighteen unless you are just already phenomenally talented; you need to be of a certain maturity so you can go after yourself as great actors have to do and strip away a lot of stuff that, at eighteen, you are too vulnerable to let go of. And once you've done that, Hollywood doesn't want it; it doesn't look good on camera, it looks fake, it doesn't work.

Some film actors are interested in theatre because they discover how interesting it is. Whether they can do it once they discover their interest is another question. They can certainly do some things, but there is a technical challenge to it that I have not seen most films actors meet. A lot of them appear in tiny little boxes in London in plays that allow them to do the kind of behavior and have the same relationship to the language that they have in film. But how many of them can do Shakespeare?

Of course, the other side of that is when you catch things on camera by improvising that are incredibly alive and in the moment. Some of the great moments in film have been invented on the spot by these unbelievably great actors.

But, as a result, the relationship to language is really different among film actors. There's a phenomenon (which, of course, I am horrified by) where people came in to audition for the film of *Angels* — some really good, young actors — and they just started improvising. One well-known young actor, very talented, was literally just inventing the whole scene, adding in all this stuff. And Mike Nichols was great. He sat there sort of staring, and the guy said, "Are you seeing anything that you don't like or anything else you want to see?" And Mike was very pleasant, but he said, "Well, I'd like to see you go back to your room and learn the script."

The actors who were cast — Al Pacino, Meryl Streep, Emma Thompson, Mary Louise Parker, Ben Shenkman, Jeffrey Wright — are all people of the theatre, as is Mike. They all had enormous respect for the text. Pacino showed up for the first day of rehearsals not with the film script but with the two paperbacks of the play. And they read and reread those, notes all over them. You want them to work from the text.

The Talent Drain

You can't cast a play in New York anymore, even a commercial play. It used to be that if you could get through the pilot season, you could do almost anything. At this point, cable is year-round and there is so much work in film that casting and rehearsing a show is impossible. Under the equity contract, you have to let people out of any rehearsal if they find something that pays more. So everybody is always popping in and out to do *Law & Order* episodes. You're left with Swiss cheese.

And forget doing what we should do, which is to rehearse for three months, as they do in Europe. I always advise people to come to a show at the end of the run. By that point, the actors have lived in it long enough to start to be able to do it. But what we usually do is watch them go through what is really the second half of the rehearsal period.

And we have a real shortage of great directors in the theatre. They are sucked dry by the time they are forty. It's horrible; it's exhausting to do. They are treated a lot better in films. It's harder work in some ways, but they don't have to do everything and they get paid a lot.

But I don't know that it has done as much damage to playwriting. I mean, I'm not somebody who could be a screenwriter if I wanted to. Those are not my talents. Suzan-Lori Parks may wind up writing great films because I think she is an incredibly great writer, but there's no question she is a playwright and second to none. It's amazing how few important playwrights have become good screenwriters. Very few. It's a different imagination; it's a different kind of response. Theatre is a tradition that has its own unique body of writers.

Film Is Our Heritage

In this country, at this particular point in history — and it has been this way for a very long time — as powerful as television is, film is the most significant art form. Going to the movies, you know, that is our heritage. This country invented them, basically, and we invented the system that made them what they are, and the whole world is crazy for them and we are crazy for them too. So when you go to the movies as an American, you are part of that tradition in some of the same way that British audiences know they are stepping into the same theatre where *Hay Fever* was first performed, in the same town where *Hamlet* was first performed. I felt that very, very powerfully the first time I worked in England. You meet people whose grandparents were actors and they are actors now. It is a legitimate profession and it has been around for a very, very long time. And you meet an old actor at the Hampstead Theatre who worked with Gielgud, Scofield, and Richardson and even older than that, and it stretches back so it's like being one breath away from a figure like Shaw.

Making Texts

I'm a playwright, so what I do is the only thing in theatre that has a shot at being permanent. But then again, what I write is sort of writing and sort of not. If you are a great genius like Shakespeare or Beckett or Brecht or Chekhov, your work has taken the form of literature. But even there, *Hamlet* — which is the greatest thing anybody has ever written — is one thing when you read it but, when you see a great *Hamlet*, is something completely different on stage. It's on the page and it's not. A really great actor will both make you aware of the literary text that's being delivered and also completely believe that you are hearing spontaneous utterance in the moment. It's impossible to settle on, but it is incredibly exciting because what they do is re-create in the moment the moment in which the text was first taken from the air and put down on paper. And that's great.

One of the things I love about writing for the stage — which is missing from screenwriting — is that you write remembering that O'Neill and Shakespeare and Shaw and Beckett and Chekhov came before you. Even if you are a middling playwright, those are your forebears, that's your antecedent form. And what you write can be read. It isn't often, but it can be. So you do write for publication as well as for the stage, and it's a text that, very importantly, actors will read as readers before they try to do it. You're creating a text that is both a score for a kinetic event and a literary text. So you carry this burden. It gives you not just the pleasure of authority — although, God knows, there is that — but a responsibility: it forces you to be good, as good as you can be, because it matters so much.

Narrative vs. Dialectic

I have always said that the art of making a movie is a very narrative-driven art that feels much more to me like writing a novel. The novel works directly with the reader's imagination so it has a virtually limitless feel; it has the ability to narrate vastness and power or incredible intimacy and microscopic detail. And film actually replicates that: in this age of the manipulation of images, it is becoming increasingly true that you can do literally anything on film. So the unfolding of narrative is — at this point in history, anyway — pretty much the work of film and novel fiction.

Whereas I don't actually think that drama has ever been about narrative; it's about dialectic. This is why we call it drama. It's a clash of ideas, a clash of forces, and it's about contradiction and the creative consequence of powerful forces locking horns.

And if you work in narrative realist drama the way that I do, the story that you tell is very important, but it's something you hang the dialectic on; it is in some ways less important. Playwrights in general through history have been less gifted as storytellers, as the creators of new fictions, than they have been as spinners of dialectics. I don't mean "spin" in the modern sense, along the lines of faking things, but setting a dialectic in motion and keeping it spinning so that it doesn't resolve until it's done. Or maybe it doesn't ever resolve because it is unrecoverable.

Reality and Illusion

At its very, very deepest heart, what theatre is most intensely about is the conflict between reality and illusion. Whereas that conflict is something that film has spent its entire history advancing away from through technology. From almost the very beginning, since Edison filmed the locomotive, film has had a way of disguising illusion successfully so that the conflict between reality and illusion doesn't get put into play. But there is no way to escape that conflict in theatre. And the greatest workers in the theatre are the people who embrace that because it's actually not a limitation of the form, but is rather the form's absolute strength and, in fact, its heart.

Of course, there are filmmakers who have played with illusion and reality: Bergman did it and Kubrick and Fellini did it. A lot of the avant garde in the '60s and '70s certainly played around with it and people are starting to again. You see it in Charlie Kaufman's screenplays, which have an element of what I would call theatricality.

But in theatre, it is inescapable. It is a challenge for the artist and a challenge for the audience, and that challenge is productive of an important way of understanding the world because theatre teaches critical consciousness. In theatre, everything that you see both is and isn't what it appears to be.

Theatre teaches that one must approach what one sees with a sharp eye toward the forces that went into creating it. It teaches one to look at the world as an artificial contraption and as an interpretation. You are never allowed not to see that when you are watching a stage play because it always fails in its task of creating illusion, no matter that the illusion may be gone after with the most astonishing ingenuity. That, to me, is the thrill of it, and the theatre artists whom I most admire are those who, like Shakespeare and Brecht, make that so much a part of their aesthetic.

When we did *Angels* at the National Theatre, the angel swung in on a rope. Someone said, "I'm worried about that. Couldn't it be a thinner wire or something?" But that is the point, because the excitement of the moment is this supernatural thing happening and, as corny as it sounds, on some level you know that that wire is there and on some level you believe it.

In *A Midsummer Night's Dream*, Act 5 Scene 1, right after Theseus and Hippolyta have discovered the lovers in the forest and the lovers wake up and tell them this bizarre story, Hippolyta says [*quoting from memory*], "Tis strange, my lord, that these lovers speak of." And Theseus answers, "More strange than true," and goes on about how we can be deceived by imagination. And then she says,

> "But all the story of the night told over,
> And all their minds transfigured so together,
> More witnesseth than fancy's images
> And grows to something of great constancy,
> But, howsoever, strange and admirable."

That power of the shared dream makes something that is not real and is real at the same time. That is theatre.

The Lessons of Theatre

Theatre throws you the three most important lessons in life. One is critical consciousness — the understanding that common "horse sense" is always part of a reactionary project to oppress and destroy people; "That's the way it is because that's the way it is." That attitude is antithetical to theatre. That's Shakespeare's joke with the mechanicals in *A Midsummer Night's Dream*: they approach a play that way. They worry the lion will scare the ladies even if it is a bad actor in a yellow yarn wig. They are completely credulous, and credulity is the antithesis of the theatrical. So that's one important lesson.

The second lesson is about loss. Theatre vanishes in front of you; you cannot recapture it. You can see a play that you love twenty-five times and what you come to realize is you are seeing a different play every single night.

And that leads you to the third lesson, which is the unbelievably powerful partnership between an audience and the staged event. The audience comes in and forms itself into a single entity in a matter of seconds — people who are strangers, who have never met. Well, it is not actually a single entity, but it has a very powerful personality. And that personality enters into this wild, intense, complicated negotiation with the people on stage, and they are guided by you and you are guided by them. It's such a lesson in things that I think are so important in the world: for instance, that we are less individual than we think — which is not to say that we are all alike, but that our boundaries are much more permeable than we realize. And the intelligence of an audience also lets you understand, I think, that people in groups sometimes function worse than people individually, but then sometimes better. There can be a virtue in collective decision making and collective engagement. That possibility of response means that you are not there simply to partake of it; you are actually the point of it in a certain way, and it is so much a give and take that if you have had a good experience at the theatre, you leave feeling just incredibly full of your own humanity. And in this increasingly creepily pornographic and fetishistic world, that is becoming a rare experience.

Ritual Sacrifice

There are ways in which the ritualistic origins of the theatre still manifest. A stage actor's job in a certain sense has to do with suffering for hire. It is an extremely difficult thing to do and it puts immense demands on the people who do it. People pay to see Fiona Shaw go through that hellacious role when she does *Medea*; Brian Cox doing *Titus Andronicus*; John Lithgow, Eileen Atkins, and Ben Chaplin doing *Retreat from Moscow*; or Tonya Pickens doing *Caroline*. Stunning: very painful, beautiful, and really, really just amazing. I mean, that's not faked. And you know while you are watching it that they are finding it inside themselves to go through that every single night. It's a little bit like killing the bull; there's a part of the human spirit that needs a surrogate. It is even true in great comic performances — you recognize the difficulty and skill of it. That is expected in a certain sense of all artists, but actors do it on their feet in front of you every single night. And everybody's watching it; everybody's minds transfigure together. It's profound, and it tells us something about ourselves that is, I think, the deepest and the most powerful and most un-ignorable aspect of human beings, which is our incredible genius for connectedness and for boundaryless-ness.

Index

Homebody/Kabul, 52, 59, 149, 154, 155
    acting in, 53, 54, 55, 56, 103, 107, 108
    audiences, 58, 59

L

L. A., *see* Los Angeles
Lahr, Bert, 110
Landscape of the Body, see Guare, John
Lane, Nathan, 94
Lange, Jessica, 43
Language, *see also* Actors, language, sensitivity
    to; Actors, text, relationship to; Text
    appreciation of, 46
    devaluing of, 89-90, 121, 147
    degradation of, 68, 126, 132, 154-155
    film vs. theatre in, 58, 150; *see also*
        Theatre, image vs. language in
    heightened, *see* Theatre, essential qualities
        of, heightened language
    landscape of, 64, 129
    opera, in, 46
    screen, on, 45, 50, 125–126, 128
La Règle du Jeu, 15
Laughter, 58, 74, 80, 88, 91, 93, 98, 110
Laughton, Charles, 15, 154
Lavey, Martha, 23–28
Law & Order, 31, 103, 151,157
Law, Jude, 85
Lear, see Shakespeare, William, King Lear
Lecompte, Elizabeth, 154
Leigh, Mike, 10, 12, 65
Lennix, Harry, 51
Lepage, Robert, 52, 120
Lester, Adrian, 73–76
Leveaux, David, 61–68
Lewinsky, Monica, 77
Lewis, C. S., 147
Lincoln Center, The, 96
Lincoln-Douglas debates, 128
Linney, Laura, 117
Lion King, The, 30, 43, 44, 45, 51, 109
Listening, 128, 130
    actors, 26, 38, 54, 75
    audiences, 8, 70, 71, 116, 129–130, 147,
        155
Literalness, 3, 4, 65; *see also* Naturalism;
    Realism; Theatre, essential qualities of,
    alienation; Theatre, essential qualities of,
    metaphor
    film, in, 4, 43, 44, 50, 81, 121, 122
    television, in, 76
    theatre, in, 4, 5, 6, 52, 64, 146
Lithgow, John, 161
Liveness, *see* Theatre, essential qualities of,
    liveness

Livent, 30
Lolita, see Nabokov, Vladimir
London, 1, 4, 18, 21, 23, 66, 89, 91
Lord of the Rings, The, 150, 151, 153
Los Angeles, 18, 76, 77, 88; *see also* Geography
    audiences, 58–59, 77
    directing in, 77
    lawyers, 64
    living in, 18, 26, 34, 76, 88
    riots, 127
    talent pool, 97
    theatre in, 77, 97-98
Love scenes, 56
Lucas, Craig
    Dying Gaul, The, 103
    Small Tragedies, 59, 155
Ludlam, Charles, 9, 10
Luhrman, Baz, 39
Lyric Opera, The, 77
Lyricism, 38

M

MacArthur "genius" fellowship, 123
Macbeth, see Shakespeare, William
Machinal, see Treadwell, Sophie
macLiammóir, Micheal, 19
Macready, William, 80
Madden, John, 16
Made-for-TV movies, 23
Madness of King George, The, see Bennett,
    Alan
Mahabharata, the, 46, 51
Mahoney, John, 23
Malkovich, John, 24, 27
Malle, Louis, 7
Maloney, Michael, 145
Mamet, David, 88, 91, 109, 133, 135
Man for All Seasons, A, see Bolt, Robert
Marat-Sade, 13
Marber, Patrick, 85–92
    After Miss Julie, 86
    Closer, 85, 90, 92
    Dealer's Choice, 85
    Howard Katz, 85
Marden, Brice, 123
Marie and Bruce, see Shawn, Wallace
Marketing, 36, 92, 94, 95, 11, 127; *see also*
    Film, marketing of
Marshall, Thurgood, 124
Mark Taper Forum, The, 53, 77, 97, 107
    Ahmanson Theatre, 77, 98
Masks, 6, 45
Master Builder, The, see Ibsen, Henrik
McCrory, Helen, 145
McDonalds, 19, 78